GENTLE YOGA FOR SENIORS, BEGINNERS AND HESITANT MEN

37 EASY LOW-IMPACT POSES & STRETCHES TO IMPROVE POSTURE, FLEXIBILITY, BALANCE AND STRENGTH

ADRIAN ROSE

MAZLOWE PUBLISHING

CONTENTS

Claim these FREE GIFTS now

As a thank you for purchasing my book (or kindly sharing it with others), I'd like to offer all of you **TWO** Free Gifts that you can access now from the link below.

#1 Yoga Planner
#2 Print-ready poses from this book and more

Why are these resources useful?

- Keep a weekly yoga journal to track progress
- No need to memorise the poses
- Only print the poses you want
- Create your own personalised yoga sequence, mix them up whenever you feel like it
- No need to flip through the pages looking for the right pose

https://tinyurl.com/AdrianRose

CLAIM YOUR FREE GIFT + USEFUL INFORMATION

Here is the link to claim your Free Gifts:

https://tinyurl.com/adrianrose

Here is the link to a very helpful and fantastic Facebook community:

https://www.facebook.com/groups/beginneryogaposes

1

INTRODUCTION & WHY YOU HAVE MADE THE RIGHT DECISION

There are some things in life we can do nothing about, and the onset of old age is one of them. Grey hairs, wrinkles and forgetting where we left the remote control are all signs that we are getting on a bit in years. Time stops for nobody.

But the thing is, nobody said *we* have to stop. Just because you're getting older doesn't mean you have to accept growing weak and frail. Loss of muscle mass, bone density, joint problems and chronic disease issues–these can be tackled if you take the right steps. And the beautiful part is–it's not too late, even if you *are* closing the gap to a 100.

We all know what it's like to ache in places that have never ached before. Bending down to pick something up can turn into a bit of an event. We take our time climbing steps, stiffness and occasional pain become familiar companions. We might feel the need to lie down after a bit of housework.

What if there was something that allowed us to retain flexibility, reduce pain, keep energy levels up and even improve our mood? Because there is one form of exercise that we can do, no matter our age, current physical condition and without an expensive gym membership, and we're going to tell you about it in this book.

With just 10-15 minutes of low impact 'exercise' per day, you'll be able to not only slow down but reverse some of the effects of ageing. And that 'exercise' is gentle yoga. I have put the word exercise in quotation marks because what we're going to show you, isn't even going to feel like exercise. What's interesting about yoga is that it has been called a 'moving meditation'. What do we associate with meditation? I'm thinking calmness, tranquillity and relaxation. Who knew that you could relax whilst exercising!?

MY EXPERIENCE

My own introduction to yoga began when I was in my teens. I injured my right knee playing football, tearing the ligaments pretty badly. My knee never properly healed, and the next injury included both ligament and cartilage damage. I had surgery to remove a bone from the joints but continued to damage the knee during full contact sport. I was young, loved football and thought I was invincible. But after months on crutches and long chats with my doctor, I had to change my sporting ambitions.

Whilst visiting my local library, back in the days before the internet arrived and we had all the information in the world at our fingertips, I came across a book on yoga. It interested me for two reasons. Firstly, because some exercises were about strengthening joints, and whilst I knew I couldn't engage in vigorous sport again, I wanted to protect what I had.

The other reason was that I was studying for exams to enter university at the time and was feeling under a lot of stress. Some of the descriptions for the poses mentioned how calming they were, allowing the energies to move through the body.

So that's how I got started, with a library book, an old exercise mat I rescued from my parent's garage, and my own body. And to be perfectly honest, thirty years on, not much has changed. I have bought a new mat, occasionally use the internet instead of my books, and I still have my body (though naturally, it has a bit more wear and tear), but I have pretty much learnt all the poses I need to know.

I'm not a yoga teacher. I've never twisted my body into a pretzel shape. I'll never do a handstand scorpion or a crow pose. I've accepted at this stage that I'm probably never going to stand on my head, and I'm okay with that.

But I do know my pigeon pose from my downward dog. I'll roll out my mat and greet the morning with a cat-cow and a half cobra. I know enough poses to keep my routine varied, and those 10-15 minutes put me in good stead for the day ahead.

To use a car analogy for a second–I would have been in the scrapyard by now if I hadn't discovered yoga. Without that book, it would have been like never going to a garage, changing the oil or getting any servicing done. Yoga allowed me to 'lubricate' my joints, deal with rust, and repair parts that were in danger of falling off. I'm probably more of a Volkswagen Beetle, one careful owner with a few miles on the clock, but I'm much loved and looked after. I won't turn heads like the Jaguar E-Type that speeds past me, but I'm happy to tootle along and confident that, with the right care going forward, I'll be able to add a few more miles to my clock. Maybe I'll pass some of those faster motors down the road as the confused driver looks under the bonnet, steam rising, and tries but fails to understand the problem. I'll give him a wave.

I have attended classes with several teachers over the years, but I've always retained my solo practice. It's become as much a part of my daily routine as brushing my teeth, essential for both my mental and physical health.

And although I'm not a teacher, I am living proof of the benefits that simple yoga poses can bring. My knee has never required further surgery and I haven't injured it since. I can walk freely without pain, and my knee feels strong. Oh, I also passed those exams and yoga has become an integral part of my stress-busting measures.

When I underwent surgery, the doctor did warn me of the increased chances of osteoarthritis in my knee when I reached middle age. I've now reached that point, and although there are no problems so far (probably because of my routines), I'm confident that with yoga, I can negate some of the symptoms if they occur.

In this book, we'll show you how you can make yoga part of your daily routine, starting at any age and from any physical starting point. With just 10-15 minutes of gentle practice each day, you can bring significant benefits to your life.

WHAT IF I'M TOO OLD OR HAVE TOO MANY ACHES AND PAINS?

I'm a bit of an evangelist when it comes to preaching the benefits of yoga, and this is a common refrain I hear when I suggest to someone that they should at least try yoga. But to me, it's a bit like saying you don't want to exercise because you're carrying too much weight. Being old, or having aches and pains, is no impediment to gentle yoga. In this book, we'll include as many options to modify regular poses as we possibly can, so that those of you who are unable to weight bear, have certain physical ailments or find it difficult to do any exercises standing up, could also benefit from yoga.

It is paramount that you consult your physician before embarking on any new exercise routine, including yoga. Even though we talk about gentle yoga and the dangers of a sedentary lifestyle can often be more consequential than getting your body moving, it is important that you give your doctor a call. There may be some poses or stretches that you should avoid altogether. We'll briefly look at some common health issues in Chapter 7 of this book and explore how yoga can still benefit you.

Please do not proceed before you've spoken to your doctor if you've ever had any of the following: any health concerns, surgery or stroke; high blood pressure or cholesterol, heart problems, obesity; suffer from any medical conditions such as an autoimmune disease; take any prescription medications; if you smoke; or have had any sort of health-related issues whatsoever in the past or present.

I INTRODUCED MY MAM TO YOGA AT 50 – 28 YEARS AGO

My mam was in her late fifties, working in a textile factory, when I first introduced her to yoga. Sitting down for long periods wasn't good for her, so I suggested that she might want to try it. I had been singing the praises of yoga to all who would listen, and despite being hesitant as she'd done no exercise since leaving school, she joined a class for local women.

My mam is now 78, and though that small class has long since ended, she has kept up her practice and now attends a much bigger class twice a week in the local community centre. A lot of the yoga she does now is based on a chair, as some of the students are in their eighties and it can be tricky getting up and down from the mat. It's gentle, it's regular and most importantly of all–it works.

As the saying goes, the proof is in the pudding. You'd never believe my mam was 78–she's spritely, energetic and full of life. She can roll out the mat or sit on a chair at home and practise, as she did during the pandemic, but she loves the social aspect of her classes. Like anyone her age, she has aches and pains and adjusts her practice accordingly. When I see the impact yoga has had on my mam's life, I'm confident about the impact it can have on the lives of others. But I know we are built differently, which leads me to my next point.

PARAMETERS

I tend to think that you should live the best life you can with the parameters you have, and I believe the same applies to yoga. Exercise according to what you can cope with, not anyone else.

I've attended a number of classes over the years, but the teachers have always delivered the same message: ONLY DO WHAT YOU CAN DO. We know our own limitations.

Proper form and technique are essential to ensure the safety and effectiveness of a yoga practice. Throughout the book, we're going to include some gentle yoga exercises to get you started. Although they are simple, we all have different bodies and conditions, so as I mentioned before, please consult with your physician if you have concerns about any exercise routines–and if it feels beyond you, don't do it.

For each of the exercises, wear loose clothing, use an exercise mat with a standard wooden kitchen or desk chair, or a fold-up metal chair–you want a chair on a surface that is solid and doesn't move. A sofa or armchair won't work as you're likely to fall asleep, and you want your body to be balanced and poised. As of yet, we haven't designed a bed yoga book.

It should also be pointed out that yoga is non-secular and does not consider any particular religious belief as a requirement for the practice, and one does not need to forgo any faith to benefit from yoga.

And one last important thing: yoga should be fun.

WHAT YOU'LL LEARN FROM THIS BOOK

We're going to cover several topics in this book that you will hopefully find informative and help you see the importance of making yoga a part of your life.

We'll look at exercise, it's vital role in keeping us fit, and how it helps with existing conditions, mobility issues, weaker bones and problems with ageing. We will show you that yoga won't inflame any current conditions but will in fact help alleviate pain associated with chronic conditions, including back pain. All claims will of course be backed by scientific studies and a few notes on personal experience.

We'll discover why it's never too late to begin exercising and how just 10-15 minutes of gentle yoga each day can become a basis for you to live independently into an old age. This is because yoga can help with sarcopenia (the medical term for muscle loss and the decline of strength and function as we age) and help maintain and even regain bone density (which is important when it comes to avoiding serious injuries).

We'll look at the dangers of a modern, sedentary lifestyle and how we can fight them, starting today. It has resulted in many of us staying on the couch more, and as we age, it can be harder to summon the energy to get moving. It will become clear how incorporating gentle yoga into our days can help us feel more vital and invigorated.

Science shows that even older adults who haven't worked out before, have the same ability to build muscle as an athlete who has continuously exercised for many years. Therefore, you have just as much to gain from exercise starting now, than someone who has been at it for years. Whilst we're not going to be building a ton of muscle here, consistent yoga practice does strengthen muscles, bones and joints over time.

After we understand the vital role gentle yoga can play in our lives, we need to tackle the problem of turning it into a habit so we can stick with it. We will discover some hacks to make yoga something you can look forward to, rather than come up with an excuse not to, and successfully make it a part of your daily routine.

We'll talk about why low-impact, gentle yoga is the most accessible form of exercise, regardless of age or medical conditions. We'll cover topics of warming up, deep breathing and mindfulness.

We'll look at the critical part that deep breathing can play in helping with anxiety and how breathing properly during your yoga poses can help remove stresses and tensions from your body.

We'll introduce you to a variety of poses that can be practised both on the chair and the mat, modified according to your specific conditions or abilities.

Last but not least, we'll talk about its numerous benefits, including but not limited to:

Increased mobility to live independently into an old age, or reach for that top shelf PB without needing to lie down after;

Better stability and balance to prevent falls;

More strength to prevent fatigue and tackle daily chores, or play with your grandchildren;

Improved flexibility to avoid pain in your muscles and joints;

Reduced levels of stress and improved emotional well-being to prevent developing depression or anxiety, and improve mental health;

Better posture and correct alignment to avoid injuries and adopting 'old folks' posture;

Better circulation around the body to promote production of joint fluid to keep joints healthy and pain-free;

Better sleep quality as the lack of good sleep has been linked to increased risk of Alzheimer's disease, and to tackle insomnia. I could go on.

With this book, we hope to show you that with just 15 to 20 minutes of gentle yoga every day, you can improve mobility and balance, manage pre-existing conditions, and ultimately feel better, healthier and more energetic. Just because we're getting older doesn't mean we have to sacrifice good health–I find that yoga is the ultimate anti-ageing tool.

So, let's move on to the next chapter, where we'll look at the vital role exercise plays in allowing us to enjoy life at all ages. We'll introduce you to one of the most essential foundational poses of any yoga practice, the Mountain Pose.

2

WHAT HAPPENS WHEN YOU MIX OLD AGE AND EXERCISE? YOU'LL BE SHOCKED

There's a school football pitch near where I live that I occasionally pass when I'm out for a walk. On the wall that runs the length of the pitch, in large white letters, is written–*We don't stop playing because we grow old; We grow old because we stop playing.*

These words are by the Irish dramatist George Bernard Shaw, and I don't think he'd mind me saying that they are just as applicable to exercise, which at its best is a form of play.

Once we get older, we're all too familiar with the changes that take place in our bodies. We become less flexible, and our marathon times become a bit slower. You sigh as another Olympics passes by and you miss the cut. Muscle loss (sarcopenia) and bone loss (osteopenia) occur as we get older. We notice that we lose balance occasionally, and when rising up from our favourite armchair to go and get another biscuit from the kitchen, we can feel a bit stiff and sore. And one of the inevitable consequences of lower energy levels as we get older is that we just don't feel like exercising.

As we progress through this book, we'll include references to research, to back up the points we are making. There have been countless studies done that provide statistical evidence of the very things we are talking about here.

This study[1] highlights the role of exercise in inflammation and chronic disease. The clinical consequences of inactivity include obesity, osteoarthritis, heart disease and asthma, dementia and depression, to name but a few. I won't add any more as I don't want to add to feelings of depression. I think we can generally agree that lack of exercise can impair our overall quality of living. I'm hoping that one of the reasons you are reading this book is that this is something you already know, and you are hoping to do something about it. Welcome; you're in the right place.

But let's start immediately with the good news. Although these things may be happening, it is possible to protect what we have and even reverse some of the effects!

BUT I'M MUCH TOO OLD TO START EXERCISING!

This is a common refrain, especially from those who haven't exercised since they closed their gym bag on their last day of school, or when they invented the TV remote. For some people, their only exercise is a quick dash to the bar when last orders are called, or an extra few steps down the far aisle of the supermarket because there's a reduction on a multi-pack of crisps. But the truth is, and something that we will emphasise throughout this book–you are never too old to exercise.

A study[2] conducted by the University of Birmingham in the United Kingdom looked at two groups of men–those over 60, who had exercised twice a week for over 20 years, and those who didn't have a regular routine. Both groups were tested before and after a weight training session and the results showed that both groups had the same ability to build muscle after exercising.

But don't worry–we're not asking you to join a gym and lift weights. This is another of the great things about yoga–all you need is your own body weight and gravity to provide all the resistance you need. It's one of the most economical and accessible forms of exercise around.

I should say at this point that if you're able for high-impact exercise–running, jumping jacks or tennis–good for you. But those aren't options for everyone, especially those of us with joint pain, who can't run the risk of injury. As much as we would love to be doing every possible type of exercise, at some stage you have to listen to what your body is telling you and accept that it takes a bit longer for injuries to heal, so there's no point jeopardising what you already have.

The beauty of a low-impact exercise such as yoga is that it allows us to get the body moving and bring many benefits of exercise, whilst also preserving our precious joints. The stretching that comes from yoga allows us to reduce the pressure on joints, keeping them loose and healthy. We can do so much to improve flexibility and suppleness, balance and strength.

This alarming study[3] delivers the startling conclusion that *110 000 deaths per year could be prevented if US adults aged 40 to 85 years or older increased their moderate to vigorous physical activities by a small amount (i.e., 10 minutes per day).* That's an extraordinary figure, don't you think? What the previous two studies have shown us is that it's never too late to start exercise, and just ten to fifteen minutes of a regular yoga routine can bring significant benefits!

That's ten to fifteen minutes between breakfast and turning on the TV in the morning. That's ten minutes before you settle into the couch to watch your favourite TV shows in the evening. Ten minutes when you come back from the shops and are thinking about starting to prepare your evening meal.

BUT IS YOGA CONSIDERED EXERCISE?

Although it's not aerobic exercise like running or swimming, it is still considered exercise, although somewhat less intense, as your heart rate is considerably lower. Which is why we've given the name 'gentle yoga' to the exercises–and we think you'll find that you will be able to see the benefits yourself after a few practice sessions.

The American College of Sports medicine[4] defines physical fitness as the sum of 'cardiorespiratory fitness, muscular strength and endurance, body composition and flexibility, balance, agility, reaction time and power', and some of their recommendations include improving fitness via flexibility and neuromotor exercise training (balance, agility and coordination). I think it'll become clear that yoga certainly helps with those.

The good thing about yoga, which I'll get into more in the next chapter, is that we are all operating from different baselines–you may be carrying injuries, have an underlying condition or are not just as flexible as you used to be. This is the beauty of yoga–it's open to everyone.

So, if you're new to exercise, you may find that yoga is more than enough for you. It may be that you quickly find that the exercises have become too easy for you–that's great! You can adjust the intensity, increase the frequency–it's your body, so you'll know what you're fit for. You might surprise yourself. Think of today as the first day of your fitter, healthier life!

ISN'T YOGA COMPLICATED?

Absolutely not. You will certainly not be expected to transition from a downward dog to a half pigeon, followed by a cobra and a cat-cow, whilst doing a supine twist in-between a one-legged crow and a dancing monkey (I made the last one up).

The yoga poses you will find in this book are simple and easy to repeat. They are the basic poses you will find in most beginner yoga studios and classes. The great thing about them is that you can repeat them or hold them for longer, depending on your own capabilities.

I personally have found that I have a core repertoire of around 20-25 poses. I have found that this range of poses has proved more than enough for me to maintain a healthy yoga routine, allowing me to feel a range of benefits. And they must be working because I've been practising for 30 years now. The proof is in the pudding, as the saying goes, and it will be the same for you as you begin to practice and start to feel the wonderful benefits of yoga in your own body and mind.

WON'T EXERCISE MAKE MY EXISTING CONDITIONS WORSE?

People with arthritis, osteoporosis or other conditions worry that exercise will make things worse for them, resulting in more pain. The truth is that the opposite is true.

The best way to think of exercise is to use the analogy of adding oil to a rusty wheel. When you don't exercise, you aren't lubricating the joints, thus making them worse. As the saying goes, use it or lose it. Low impact exercises, such as the gentle yoga techniques we are highlighting in this book, are the equivalent of adding lubrication to the joints, allowing them to work better.

The key to gaining benefits from yoga or indeed, any exercise is consistency–it's taking ten to fifteen minutes every day and practising some simple techniques that won't result in unnecessary strain or pain. And it's worth repeating again–if you're feeling pain, don't continue with the pose. And the opposite is also true–you may find that short periods of gentle yoga aren't enough. Feel free to add another session to your day, or practice for a little while longer. It's your body, so only you can know the impact it's having.

On the other hand, don't become so enthused that you burn out or worse, overdo it and injure yourself. It's easy to get carried away by enthusiasm when you start exercising. Although that's great and keeps you going, the important thing is not pushing yourself too far and making yoga a part of your daily regime.

A lot of success in life is achieved by just showing up. And it's often easier to say no than yes. What we are encouraging throughout this book is for you to show up on the mat, or the chair, and apply what you have learnt in this book–we think you'll be surprised at just how effective some of these techniques are. Habit forming is something we will be looking at in a later chapter.

I ACHE ALL OVER. IS THERE ANY POINT EXERCISING AT MY AGE?

Sarcopenia is the decline of strength and muscle function as we age. It's estimated that we lose between 3%-5% of muscle each decade after the age of 30, with a higher rate of decline after 60.[5] This adds to feelings of weakness and fatigue, and we're no longer as flexible as we once were. Back pain is something that can develop because core muscles are weaker, and bad posture also takes its toll. This can cause imbalances that can lead to falls, leading to broken bones or worse, something which becomes a frequent worry as we get older.

One of the most interesting studies in recent years was carried out by Dr Loren Fishman[6], a physiatrist at Columbia University, who specialised in Rehabilitative Medicine. His study looked at a link between yoga and bone density, particularly the one million spinal and hip fractures that occur yearly in the US. He wanted to see if he could establish an alternative to the drugs prescribed, which often resulted in unwanted side effects.

In a study that lasted for a decade, with over 700 participants, 200 of whom were yoga students practising regularly. The average age of the participants was 68 and over 80% of them had either osteoporosis or osteopenia (a condition which can lead to osteoporosis), for which there is no cure.

Dr Fishman recognised that because weight bearing activity is often prescribed to patients suffering from bone loss, many yoga positions met this criteria, as yoga can put more pressure on the bone than gravity does.

His results were startling.

By following a regular yoga practice, those who had experienced a gradual decline in bone density in the years leading up the study and before they started practising yoga, were in fact able to regain bone density. Stop to think about this for a moment, because it's actually quite remarkable.

Improvements were seen in the spine and the femur, and to a lesser extent, in the hip. It's also important to note that, with over 90,000 hours of yoga recorded, no fractures or injuries related to yoga were recorded, again highlighting how safe yoga is to practice.

The study supported the belief that yoga can help reverse bone loss, as well as highlighting the improvements in posture and balance that come from practising yoga. And because yoga helps with movement, strength, coordination and reducing anxiety, it can prevent you from falling in the first place, thus preventing a serious injury from a fracture.

So, there we go–the power of yoga becoming apparent again. By engaging our muscles, even if it's just for a short time each day, we can ensure that we don't lose them. And if there's a better exercise to help with bad posture, I don't believe I've found it yet. It's important to remember that flexibility is something that comes from yoga, and it will improve the more you practice. Have no doubt–a regular gentle yoga routine can contribute greatly to your overall quality of life.

I'M OLD AND I SUFFER FROM LONELINESS. WILL THIS HELP?

We all know that older people are especially vulnerable to loneliness and feelings of depression. For a variety of reasons, older people can become socially isolated, and this can have a major impact on their mental health. Perhaps retirement has reduced their circle of friends, maybe family live and work further away. According to Age UK,[7] over two million people are projected to be suffering from loneliness by 2025/26 and these figures have massive implications for health providers and society as a whole.

One of the most shocking statistics[8] I have read recently was from Age UK too, which found that 1.7 million in England can go for a month without meeting up with a friend. In this same period, over 300,000 people at age 65 and over have not even had a conversation. This made me incredibly sad, and there's no doubt loneliness is becoming an epidemic.

Of course, you can practice yoga alone, but you can also invite a friend round to do the same. Like we said previously, there's no special equipment required. Maybe you could organise for a group of you to meet at a friend's house, and combine yoga with some tea and scones? (I wouldn't suggest mixing yoga and alcohol. I don't want anyone to get injured after combining a bird dog pose with a dancing monkey. Ouch.)

Maybe you have a friend who could also benefit from a gentle yoga practice–perhaps you could start together and support each other. This could mean going to a class together or starting up your home practice at the same time. You can meet up for tea and compare notes on your downward dog–though don't be getting too competitive! One of the great things about yoga is its uncompetitive nature–everyone has a different level of ability, but each of us gets the benefits we need.

I mentioned my mam in the introduction. She's 78 years old with a twice weekly gentle yoga practice in the local community centre for an hour at a time. One of the highlights for her is meeting people in her class, so it's become an important social outlet. They even organise a Christmas dinner each year, and that's something that she really looks forward to.

Being lonely can also exacerbate feelings of anxiety and depression and this is something that yoga can also help with. Depending on which poses you practice, it can be incredibly slow and relaxing–though you can make it as fast paced as you wish. Stretching helps to release tensions that can often be stored in the body and this gentle exercise is a great way of releasing them. Exercise of any type is a great mood booster, and any amount is better than nothing at all.

When we wake up, it's easy for our minds to be carried away by the events of the coming day. Lots of little anxieties and worries start to build up even before we've got out of bed, and it's very easy to be in a mood even before your day begins.

These ten to fifteen minutes that you carve out of your day are 'your' time. They are just for you, an opportunity to relax and let go. It's hard to think of a better way of starting your day.

DO I NEED TO EAT PROPERLY TO EXERCISE?

I think it would be remiss to talk about exercise without mentioning nutrition. As we get older, we do need more protein to preserve muscle mass and bone health. However, because we tend to be less physically active as we get older, we don't need as many calories, so we eat less. Luckily, doing yoga daily increases your physical activity. But it can't be stressed enough–make sure you're getting enough protein, as it's beneficial to ageing muscle as well as bone health. Experts suggest at least 2g of protein per kg of optimal body mass per day for people over 50, whereas for younger adults, just 0.8g per kg is recommended. You see, you'll almost need to double your intake of protein as you get on a bit in years. For someone weighing around

155 pounds, or 70kg, this would be around 140 grams of protein per day.

Okay, so there you have it. I think we've covered a lot of the issues regarding exercise as we get older and hopefully answered some of your questions, as well as highlighting just how vital a role fifteen minutes of gentle yoga a day can play in helping you to not only maintain, but also improve your health.

Before I introduce you to our first pose, I want you to think about what we have just covered, and the difference it can make to your life. Maybe the ability to continue to be active with your grandchildren. To continue to be able to socialise, meet friends and take walks and holidays. To live the most active life possible, for as long as possible.

Alright, I think it's time–let's get started with a pose!

MOUNTAIN POSE

Mountain pose was one of the first poses I learnt, and I usually begin and end my practice with it before I move into Shavasana (don't worry, I'll introduce Shavasana at a later stage. It's a good one, as it basically involves lying down on the ground). It looks deceptively simple but you are actually using every muscle and it's good for bringing awareness to your body, helps improve posture and with regular practice, can help with back pain (again, if you have pain issues, consult with your doctor or a trained yoga teacher. Only stretch to a point where you feel mild tension–never stretch through pain).

If you suffer from dizziness, you might want to avoid this pose, or avoid closing your eyes, use a wall or a chair to keep you stable–or, refer to our Seated Mountain Pose instead.

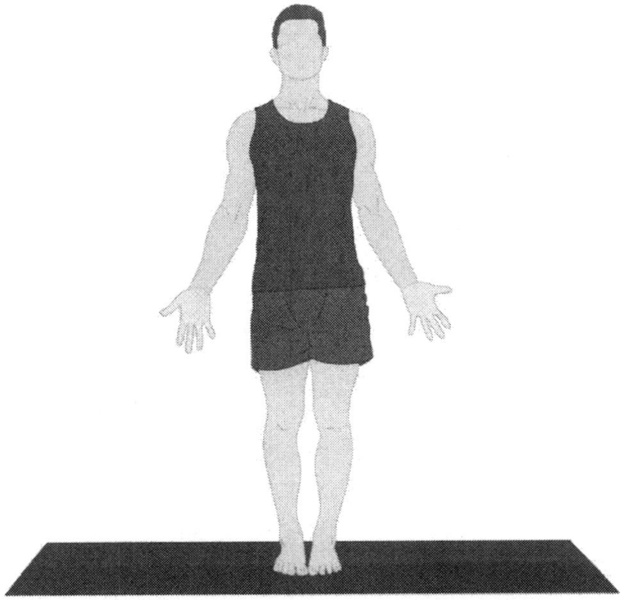

1. Stand with your feet hip-width apart or together with the base of your big toes touching, all depending on how good your balance is. If balance is a problem, keep your back against a wall. Try to keep your back straight with your arms at your side. Lift and spread your toes, then shift your weight to find the proper balance.
2. Engage the leg muscles by firming your quadriceps as you're lifting your kneecaps slightly, and lengthen your tailbone. Try to avoid locking your knees, which can place unnecessary stress on your joints, but keep your legs as straight as you can (it's called a microbend). Align your shoulder blades with your hips.
3. Lengthen your body by extending the crown of your head towards the ceiling along with your sternum, without pushing your lower ribs forward. Widen your collarbones and keep your arms at your side with your palms facing frontwards. You can also put your hands in the prayer position in front of your chest, also known as Anjali Mudra.

4. Close your eyes if you're happy with your balance. What I try to do is imagine a line of energy that begins in my feet, moves up my legs and thighs, and through my centre (the core) all the way to the top of my head. I always feel the benefit of the pose when I do this, and it also helps to keep my body straight.

The Mountain Pose improves posture and body awareness, as well as concentration. It works to strengthen and stabilise your knees, thighs, buttocks and abdomen. It can reduce stress by bringing about calmness.

Don't worry if you can't stand up or are worried about balance. We can do this in a chair as well.

SEATED MOUNTAIN POSE

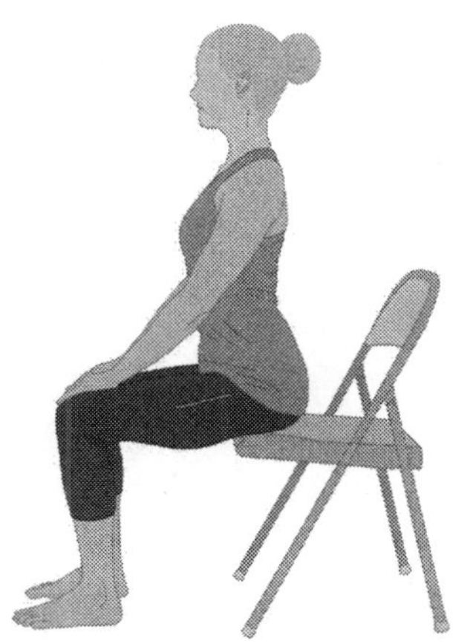

1. Try to sit towards the edge of your seat with your legs bent, and feel your feet rooted to the ground. Let your hands rest on your knees.
2. Firmly root your sitting bones into the chair. Feel how grounded this is.
3. Take a deep breath and feel this energy rising through your

body–through your pelvis, your core, your spine, all the way to the crown of your head. If you need to, rock back and forth on your sitting bones until you feel your weight is evenly distributed.

4. Keep your spine neutral and natural, not ramrod straight.
5. Keep your chin parallel to the ground, the crown of your head rising, and close your eyes or gaze straight ahead.
6. Breathe deeply, letting the energy flow up and down your body with each flow of breath. Feel free to turn your palms upward as you rest your hands on your knees or thighs.

The great thing about the Mountain Pose is that it can be done anywhere, whether you're waiting in line at the post office, taking a break from crouching over the laptop at your desk, or waiting for the kettle to boil.

Look at that! You've done your first yoga pose and started your journey into better health. And in the next section, we're going to look at all of the benefits that yoga can bring.

3

WHY EVERYTHING YOU KNOW ABOUT YOGA MIGHT BE WRONG

When an exercise like yoga has been practiced for 5000 years, you know it must have something going for it. Whilst Jazzercise classes are no longer advertised and vibrating belts lie dormant in garages, yoga remains as popular as ever. According to recent figures[1] over 300 million people practice yoga, and just in the past five years alone, yoga participation has increased by 50%. More and more people are discovering the benefits that it brings and it's not going away anytime soon.

Over the years as a practitioner, I've heard all sorts of myths about yoga, and I'm going to debunk some of those here. Maybe you've read this far into the book and still remain unconvinced, so I'm also going to list some of the many benefits of yoga.

YOGA ISN'T FOR MEN

This is one of the most repeated myths I have heard over the years. It usually comes from other men who can't see their toes, never mind touch them, because they can't see over their beer bellies. The last time they saw their knees they were probably carrying a schoolbag. Still, as a bloke, it's something I have gotten used to over the years.

Although I first started practicing by myself over thirty years ago, I have attended classes during this time, and I would always recommend them. You get to learn from a trained teacher, and they can correct you on your form and you can ask questions about poses. I also like the shared spirit in classes, especially more relaxed ones.

My first teacher was also a man, Barry, and he's still a friend of mine, and now he runs the classes that my mam attends. But in that first class, from what I remember the ratio of women to men was about 15 to 1. It didn't bother me, but I often felt it was a shame that more men weren't getting the same benefits that I was.

I have had a gym membership a couple of times over the years, but I never attended for more than a few months before I gave up. I didn't like the culture in some of them–sometimes you'd have these huge hulks stalking around the floor, throwing talc around themselves before roaring as they attempted another lift. The constant thumping house music (why is it always house music in gyms?) used to give me a headache.

That being said, it may be that I just attended the wrong gym. This was a few years ago.

I appreciate gyms have changed and are much more welcoming places for both sexes. Strength training is vitally important, and everyone wants to have the best body they possibly can. My point is that it doesn't always have to be about strength, and it's OK to think about things such as flexibility, posture, and the skeletal structure.

THE PUB

For some men, the only weight training they do is lifting pints in the pub, which was where I got into conversation with some of the local lads from my small town. They were questioning me about yoga, wanting to know about its benefits. Of course, I was able to answer all their questions, but I was curious as to why the sudden interest?

My friend Barry had the genius idea of starting a men's only class. People who haven't gone to an exercise class in many years, if even ever, are wary because they are conscious of their bodies, and don't want to make a fool of themselves if they can't do the exercises properly. They're also especially self-conscious of being in front of the opposite sex.

The reason the men had an interest in the class was because they were all golfers. Twisting and swinging had taken a toll on their bodies over the years, resulting in back and hip pain, with a range of strains, pulled muscles, disc problems, inflammation of the joints–you name it, someone had it.

I didn't play golf myself, but I was delighted to see the lads at least trying yoga, so I was happy to attend. The first few classes were small, as we only needed a small space. One of the participants owned a pub, and he had a spare room above that he used for small functions, so there were about ten of us that used it.

It was a cramped room, and our mats were basically touching. Some of the men were moving body parts that hadn't been stretched in a long time, and I heard noises that sounded like they came from small animals that were stuck somewhere and couldn't get out. The last time I had heard such moans and groans was on a ghost train I'd been on during a school trip. I remember at one stage the beginner yogi beside me doing a reclined spinal twist and hitting me in the face with his outstretched arm.

The first few weeks were tough going, and a few dropped out. But word began to spread. Back pains that physios had worked on to no avail, and that drugs could only partially help with, were suddenly much better. Some found that they could swing without feeling any pain for the first time in years. I should say at this point that as far as I'm aware, none of their golf games improved, but I never said yoga was a miracle cure. But that was irrelevant, because for the men the main thing was to be out on the greens a couple of times a week, playing golf with their friends, and not suffering because of it.

Through word of mouth, attendance at the men's only classes improved. Soon, due to space issues, they had to move into the larger community space. Such was the popularity, the men and women's class merged, and although there were still more women, the ratio was more like 70/30. But the men were now confident enough to attend the mixed sex classes.

The classes are still going–two nights a week now. In a small town, once word gets around about the benefits of something like yoga, others turn up to see what the fuss is all about. I've moved, but sometimes when I visit my mam for a few days, I take my mat and attend a class. Which brings me nicely to one of the many benefits of yoga.

YOU DON'T NEED FANCY EQUIPMENT

No expensive gym membership, free weights or expensive machinery needed here. A good yoga mat, some loose clothing–that's all you need. Though if you are a man and are attending classes, maybe wear something other than loose gym shorts. There are some things that can slip out in certain poses, and nobody really wants to see that. Loose clothing but long enough to stay covered and allow you to move freely in poses.

A chair for some of the exercises if your mobility is restricted is going to be important.

Something solid that can sit on your mat and doesn't slip is ideal.

You can buy a couple of foam blocks to help with some of the exercises, which you can pick up cheaply, but I don't use them too often. If you're able to get on the mat, they can help you reach down to some poses, bringing the ground towards you.

If you'd like to attend with others, many community classes are offered. Shop around, and you'll see that you don't have to attend expensive sessions at yoga studios.

There are also some yoga teachers on YouTube and online. These are great for practicing form and learning poses. Just remember that the teacher can't see you, so if you're worried about doing it correctly, join a class. But the simpler poses which we are featuring here shouldn't be beyond anyone–I've said it before but it's worth repeating–just don't continue if you feel pain.

So, no monthly memberships needed–gentle yoga is perfect to do within the confines of your own home. No need to get in the car and drive all the way to some far away gym that you'd prefer not to be in anyway. Just your mat in a small space at home, and a chair if needed. Modify the exercises to suit the needs of your own body.

If you fancy, you can join a Facebook community to talk yoga, perhaps even connect with others in your area to get together and start practicing. You'll find some useful links to yoga communities and online classes at the end of this book.

SO, TELL ME MORE ABOUT SOME OF THESE BENEFITS

Before we move onto another pose at the end of this chapter, let's quickly recap some of these amazing benefits yoga can provide.

Yoga can:

... lead to improved flexibility and give you a greater range of motion. One of the things you often notice with yoga when you start out is just how inflexible you are. Maybe you are bending down to tie your shoelaces and you notice a lot of stiffness. One of the great things about yoga after you have been practicing for a while is you notice how much more flexible you are becoming. You are stretching your muscles, reducing stress and tension, leaving you much more relaxed. Before you know it, you're walking down the street and you notice a pound coin on the ground. With no problems at all, you bend down and scoop it up! Something else to point out here is that the body is interconnected. Remember that old song, 'the knee bone is connected to the thigh bone, the thigh bone's connected to the hip bone' etc? Well, tight hips can often cause knee pain because the thigh and shin bones aren't properly aligned, and tight hamstrings can cause back pain because they pull on your pelvis, tilting it backwards and tilting your lower back forwards.[2]

... help with balance, thus reducing the likelihood of injuries resulting from falls. It also helps speed up recovery if you are unfortunate enough to suffer from a fall.

... improve your posture, so you're less likely to suffer from pain or injuries that occur due to poor alignment–such as lower back, shoulder and neck pain.

... improve mood–exercise releases endorphins, leading to a natural high. Many of the exercises are relaxing and help with breathing, so they help to reduce stress. This in turn helps our emotional wellbeing and improves feelings of self-esteem. Yoga also helps us to remain grounded, not letting our thoughts run away, helping us to remain calm and self-aware.

... help if you are suffering from a chronic condition, it may be that yoga will help. We'll look at this in more detail in a later chapter.

... be adapted. Don't worry about your own physical limitations or disabilities–gentle yoga exercises can be modified to fit each individual's needs.

... feel natural. One of the things I've noticed over the years is how much yoga doesn't actually feel like exercise. The poses begin to feel like natural movements in the body, especially when aligned with your breathing.

... help with joints because it is low impact. No pounding the pavements with yoga or jumping up and down. It also improves circulation and improves the muscle around the joints. Yoga helps to promote Synovial (joint) fluid, which allows for smooth movement of the bones and nourishes joint cartilage.[3] The amount of joint fluid decreases as we age, which is partly why our joints get stiffer and don't move as well. The good news is that yoga is the right step towards protecting your joints.

... improve your blood flow. Don't worry, I'm not about to ask you to stand on your head. The relaxation exercises you learn through yoga help with circulation, especially your hands and feet. Your cells function better, because yoga pumps more oxygen to them, and haemoglobin and red blood cells also increase, and they carry oxygen to the muscle tissues. Some of my favourite yoga poses are twists, which act by almost wringing out our internal organs, detoxifying them. I have used them on a few occasions when I have been hungover, and they have worked an absolute treat. I'm sure this doesn't apply to you as you are very well behaved and don't touch alcohol (very wise). And don't be tempted to get drunk just so you can be hungover and test this hypothesis. Trust me, it works.

... help with sleep. Because of its relaxing qualities, this has been a big one for me, and I'll expand on this in a later chapter.

... helps you to become more aware of your body. The more that you practice, the more you become aware of your own limitations. This should act as a preventative measure, so that when you find yourself in a situation where, for example, you have to reach down to a five-pound note that's lying on the ground and you remember from your last forward fold that you have to bend your knees a little bit more to avoid hurting yourself.

... boosts the health of your heart. Rather than increasing your heart rate, gentle yoga exercises can help by relaxing your heart, by focusing on deep breathing and it also helps to reduce stress, something else that can only be good for your heart. We'll look at this a bit more in the next chapter.

Okay, so time for another exercise. I mentioned twists earlier, and about wringing out your internal organs, so how about a simple twist?

Now, if you are able to get to the ground, it's time to learn the easy pose. If not, read along for a modification of this pose for the chair. A word of warning first. If you have spinal issues, the twist isn't for you, and you'll probably want to avoid the easy pose if you have knee problems. Again, check with your physician first if you have concerns about any of these poses.

EASY POSE

Like its name suggests, the aim is to sit in this pose 'with ease' using whatever props you need. It's a relaxing, hip opening pose that's good for stretching the knees and ankles whilst also strengthening the back.

1. Sit down on your padding and cross your legs, spreading the flesh on your butt so that your sit bones have a strong foundation.
2. Imagine that the crown of your head is attached to the ceiling by a piece of thread. Move side to side and back and forth so that your shoulders are correctly aligned. Let your shoulder blades slide down your back, allowing your shoulders to move away from your ears.
3. By moving the knees closer together, you ensure that your hips are properly aligned. You can open your hips a little bit more by flexing your feet, allowing your little toes to touch the ground.
4. Let your hands rest gently in your lap.
5. Inhale deeply, letting your spine grow. With each deep breath, allow yourself to feel more rooted to the ground. Stay here for a few breaths.

Should you not be able to get on the floor or prefer to remain seated, you can start from the Seated Mountain Pose. Instead of crossing your legs on the floor, you remain seated in a chair towards the edge of the seat, with your legs firmly rooted to the ground. Then you can follow steps 2 to 6 above.

From the Easy Pose or the Seated Mountain Pose, we're going to move into a simple twist.

EASY TWIST

One of the main points to remember in any twist, is to inhale as you lengthen, exhale as you twist.

1. Inhale as you stretch your arms toward the sky. As you exhale, turn towards your right-hand side and place your right hand on the ground. The left hand can go on the outside of your right leg. Breathe deeply.
2. Inhale and return to the centre. Repeat on the other side.

This is a great pose for increasing flexibility in your chest, shoulders and spine. It also stimulates the organs, in particular your kidneys.

Don't worry if these poses feel beyond you. The whole way through, we're going to include postures that can be done sitting down. And remember, poses that seem difficult now can become easier the more you practice, and your flexibility improves.

SEATED EASY TWIST

For this one, make sure your chair is solid and on a flat surface.

1. Sit forward as much as you can towards the edge of your chair. Keep your feet flat on the ground.
2. Deep inhale as you raise your arms to the sides then up.
3. Exhale as you gently twist your lower body to the right, lowering your arms. You can rest your right arm on the back of the chair, but don't use it as leverage to force yourself into the twist. Keep your left hand resting at your side.
4. Look over your right shoulder and breathe deeply five times.
5. Return back to your central position, then repeat on the other side.

This a great pose that helps with lower back pain, easing indigestion and helping with circulation.

Alright, so that's another pose learnt! We're well on the way to becoming yogis. Now, we're going to move on to the next chapter and look at the dangers of living a sedentary lifestyle, before we move on to some more poses to help us counteract the effects of this damaging, albeit modern way of living.

4

WHY IS IT MORE DANGEROUS TO STAY SEDENTARY AND WHAT CAN YOU DO ABOUT IT NOW

There is a misconception amongst the general populace that exercise must leave you completely drained before you are able to gain any benefit from it. The idea is that unless you have virtually collapsed post workout, with sweat flooding from your pores, there's no point exercising. Of course, this is a fallacy.

Yes, there's no doubting the joys of a good workout–the feel-good endorphins pumping through your body, that feeling of complete exhaustion and the pleasure that comes from feeling totally spent. But it's not for everybody, and there are many of us who like to take things that little bit easier. It's also not the only type of exercise.

Naturally, there is a balance between working out to the point of exhaustion and doing absolutely nothing at all. Last time I checked, opening a packet of crisps is not considered exercise. Sending the dog outside and then calling it again and checking if it's wet, because you can't be bothered to get up and find out what the weather is like outside, is also quite lazy.

It's always easier to not do something, than to do something. That's just a fact of life for some people. Taking the first step isn't always easy and you can sometimes do with a bit of motivation. And knowing just how much of a devastating impact the sedentary lifestyle is having on your body is as good a place as any to start.

DANGERS OF PHYSICAL INACTIVITY

According to the World Health Organisation,[1] approximately two million deaths per year are attributed to physical inactivity. Between 60 to 85% of the world's population, in both developed and developing countries, lead lifestyles that double the risk of cardiovascular diseases, increased levels of obesity, osteoporosis, colon cancers as well as mood disorders such as anxiety and depression. What I found particularly depressing in this report was that two thirds of children aren't considered active, so you can only imagine the health tsunami that's going to be bearing down on us in future years and the impact this will have on society.

This study[2] from 2020 makes for sobering reading. As well as 15% of the world's global population not engaging in sufficient physical activities, I was shocked when I read that inactivity accounts for 6% of global mortality. The study also makes the point that lack of space and the prevalence of television in the home makes it difficult to exercise. I think it's worth repeating at this point that you don't need space to complete gentle yoga exercises as they can be done in the comfort of your own home. You can also leave the television on whilst you're exercising if you can't bear to tear yourself away from the constant breaking news or your favourite drama. Though it's quite OK to hit pause and give yourself a break too.

Obviously, we all know the importance of nutrition and quitting tobacco, but the other most important thing we can do is to get moving. Modern living has truly led to some of this, from watching so much television to playing video games and the ubiquitous use of cars meaning that we don't walk anywhere anymore. The amount of people that I see on a daily basis, driving short distances to the shops, infuriates me. I absolutely understand that we live in a world of time pressures, especially when you have a family, but you only have to look around you and see the levels of childhood obesity, and then see parents driving their children to buy junk food, that it becomes easy to make a link.

Another study in 2015[3] also makes a good point about the dangers of sitting down for too long, which has been linked to heart disease, cancer and type 2 diabetes. Sitting has been called the new smoking, such are the risks. Obviously those ten to fifteen minutes of exercise are important each day, but it's important that you are also moving around for the rest of the day.

DESK JOB

I work at a desk job, and I know how easy it is to lose track of time and suddenly find myself getting absorbed in a project and suddenly find I haven't moved in a couple of hours. Before I know it, I've found that my shoulders and neck begin to feel hunched and strained. I noticed how wound up I feel. When I realised this was happening, I made a few changes.

I have a watch that reminds me to move every hour, for a minimum of two minutes. It's just as easy to set a reminder on your phone to alert you every hour. I usually just get up and walk a couple of lengths of the corridor, go get a glass of water. Anything that gets me moving for a couple of minutes. It's probably best not to use it as a reminder to get up, walk into the kitchen, and get stuck into a multi bag of crisps.

I also stretch a lot whilst at my desk, something which I'll be featuring in this book. Sitting on the edge of my chair and doing a seated mountain pose becomes very easy. It's also incredibly easy to do a few side stretches with the arms overhead. I can almost feel the benefits of this immediately and they are an important part of my health armoury in work, which can become stressful. When I incorporate these stretches with some deep breathing, they can often make a big difference to my day. Maybe I'm coming off a stressful phone call, or about to walk into a meeting that I know is going to be difficult–these little mini breaks become an oasis of calm during my day.

Another thing that I do is when I'm on the phone, I walk and talk. Even if it's just pacing around my living room, I find it greatly beneficial. If I know I have to make a phone call during the day outside of work, I try and keep it until my lunch break. Then I can combine exercise, fresh air and being sociable. There's also something about movement that allows me to think better.

When writing this book, I came up against a couple of blocks I didn't know how to get around, usually concerning content and how it was structured. But I did what I always do when I have a problem on my mind. I set out and walk; I don't dwell on the problem, but my subconscious mind is working away in the background. Usually when I reach the end of my walk, a solution or useful suggestion has worked its way through the recesses of my grey matter into the conscious mind. This also works for me during sleep–ask yourself a question you need answered, and very often the solution has filtered through to your mind by morning. I should add that this doesn't work for the lottery numbers or the winner of the 2:45 at Chepstow.

KEEP ON MOVING

There's something about moving that helps the cognitive processes. This research[4] looks at the relationship between walking, cognitive processes and academic skills and how brain processing and plasticity are improved by as little as ten minutes of walking each day. I can say with my hand on my heart that I have found the same benefits with yoga; on many occasions I have had something heavy on mind, and very often after a session I know exactly what I have to do. I don't want to make this sound like it's some sort of supernatural ability–as the research above shows, it just allows your brain to function better.

It's important not to complete your morning exercise and then feel that you can now rest on the settee for the remainder of the day, as if in some way you have to 'earn' your place as a couch potato. That's not the right way to think. Engaging in exercise should give you more energy and encourage you to move about more. You'll want to at least walk around and tell people how good gentle yoga is, or phone your friends when you are out and about to purchase this book.

Humans aren't meant to spend so much time sitting down. Everything works better when we're standing upright. It's vital for energy levels, for bone health, for mood and our weight, and it also aids digestion. Obviously, I'm making an exception for those who are seated due to their conditions, but my point remains.

The beauty of gentle yoga, and something we'll be showing in a later chapter, is how you can immediately move into some of the exercises. Perhaps you want to stand and do a mountain pose, or do it from the edge of your chair. A side arm stretch might be in order. There's lots you can do. I have been tempted to do a downward dog in work on a couple of occasions but I'm not sure what my boss would make of it.

Although the statistics for mortality and disease relating to sedentary behaviour might be both deeply depressing and terrifying, there's lots you can do to remedy this. And reading this book can be considered one of the most important steps on that path.

SO, WHAT CONSTITUTES EXERCISE?

According to the Centers for Disease Control and Prevention (CDC) National Centre for Health Statistics,[5] only 20% of adults across the US aged between 18 and 64 meet the guidelines for both muscle strengthening and aerobic exercise, as recommended by the US federal government. The recommendation for more vigorous activities,[6] such as jogging, cycling and circuit weights, is 75 minutes per week. The recommendation for more moderate activities, which include brisk walking, and more importantly in the context of this book, yoga, is 150 minutes a week.

One hundred fifty minutes sounds a lot, right? But break that down over a week, and it's just over twenty minutes a day. That's pretty achievable, when you consider that gentle yoga alone can be done for ten to fifteen minutes at a time. When you consider the importance of this, to maintain and improve both our physical and mental health, fight disease and age-related conditions, and contribute to the longevity of our lives, I think it has to be agreed that it's not a big ask. When you consider the length of an episode of your favourite TV drama is probably thirty minutes or more, I think it might be time to reprioritise.

And like previously stated, I do appreciate that some of us are bound by existing ailments and conditions, and that's okay too, and that's the beauty of gentle yoga. We can get off the couch and get our heart rates up without having to pound the pavements or hit the gym. That's what this book is all about–inviting you to make small, regular changes that will get you doing something.

As someone wiser than me once said, a little of something is better than a lot of nothing.

So, now we've scared you with talk of the dangers of the sedentary lifestyle, time for another exercise. This one is specifically for when you've spent too much time in front of the TV and need to release some of the stagnant energy that gathers when we've been sitting for too long.

This is called the seated side stretch.

SEATED SIDE STRETCH

Be extra careful with this one if you have or have had injuries to your arm, shoulders, neck, rib cage or spine. Another point is that if you have back pain and find it difficult to sit for too long, maybe use a rolled up blanket to give your back a bit more support. If you have blood pressure issues or are prone to dizzy spells, it's probably advisable to stick to the seated positions, rather than taking to the mat. Again, check with a physician and listen to your body.

1. You're in your seat with your hands on your lap, head nicely balanced.
2. Close your eyes and take a few nice, deep breaths.
3. On an inhale, raise your right arm overhead and move it over to the left as far as you can. At the same time, tilt your neck and chin in the same direction.
4. You can exhale at this point, then take another breath, all the time feeling the stretch.
5. Inhale again and extend the right arm, bringing it back down alongside your chair whilst relaxing your neck and shoulder.
6. Repeat on the other side, this time using the left arm.

Although this pose may seem deceptively simple, it's actually really good for opening up the neck and shoulder muscles. It also lets you see the importance of breathing deeply, really feeling the stretch and opening up the diaphragm. It's one of my favourite poses because my job is mostly desk based, where I spend far too much time hunched over a computer. It really does help with bad posture. We spend so much time bent over our mobile phones or clutching our steering wheels that it's no wonder that our bodies suffer so much from poor alignment.

It's just as easy to do this pose standing up. It's not unlike the Mountain Pose that we practiced in an earlier chapter–it really helps with our breathing and we can bring ourselves to a place of quiet calm.

STANDING SIDE STRETCH

1. Stand nice and tall with your feet close together.
2. Reach both arms overhead as you take in a deep breath.
3. Lower your right arm down the right side of your body as you exhale and lengthen the left arm overhead, bending to the right.
4. Inhale as you return to the centre, repeating the exercise on the left side of your body.

5

THE EASIEST WAY TO TURN YOGA INTO A DAILY HABIT

"*An object that is at rest will stay at rest unless a force acts upon it. An object that is in motion will not change its velocity unless a force acts upon it.*"

The above statement is Newton's first law of physics. Basically, what he is saying is that objects that are moving will keep moving. Objects that aren't moving, well, they'll stay that way. Unless, in both cases, a 'force acts upon it.'

I sometimes wonder if Newtown wrote this whilst lying on a sofa on a Sunday afternoon. He'd just had his dinner, and there was a big football match about to start on the TV that he was only slightly interested in but couldn't turn off either. He just couldn't summon the energy to do anything (he might have arsed about on the internet or checked his phone twenty times, except they didn't have those things back in the 17th century).

What was the force that got him off the sofa? Perhaps his wife yelled at him that he was lying around the house and he'd promised 'he'd do something about the garden'.

Chewing the end of his quill, he reached for a piece of parchment and wrote down his first law of physics. Perhaps he then grabbed an apple, wandered into the garden and got thinking about something else.

Sitting around, our thinking becomes stagnant. We can get stuck in a cycle of rumination, thinking about doing something, but putting it off. It's possible to spend hours in this transitory state, and we can often become depressed doing so. It's easier to do nothing than something. But it is possible to break out of this state of inertia, and in this chapter, we're going to show you how. What Newton terms 'force' can come from within, which is of course where all great change begins.

JOGGING

During the lockdown of 2020, like many people, I became quite stagnant. I found I was lethargic and dull, both in body and mind. Even going for a walk became an effort, because of distance restrictions and constantly walking the same route. I was doing yoga but even that was a bit of an effort. I was lying around too much and I needed to get moving again, but I found it hard to find the motivation to do anything about it.

I decided to do something drastic by my standards. Despite not having run since I was a teenager, I decided I was going to try and move a bit faster. By now I had been free of knee pain for several years and decided to try some gentle jogging. I wouldn't be 'pounding the pavements', rather I'd be giving them a gentle caress. At the first sign of any knee problems, I'd call it quits.

I signed up for the couch to 5k programme and installed the app on my phone. I invested in a good pair of running shoes. I bought some shorts and a couple of running shirts. Invested in an all-weather running jacket. I was all ready to go.

Except I wasn't.

Those first few mornings I had a ready-made excuse. I was too tired. I'd be late for work. I didn't go in the evenings because there were too many people around. For some reason, I was self-conscious about running, because I'd put on a few pounds during lockdown and that didn't sit well with me. During this time, every time I looked out the window there seemed to be people power walking and running–it was as if everyone had decided they were going to make the Tokyo Olympics.

No, I wanted to be a morning runner. But nothing was happening.

I sat down and wrote down my motivations for running. I wanted to get rid of some cobwebs by shaking up my exercise schedule. I wanted to lose a few pounds. I needed to do something completely different.

So, I made a deal with myself. I'd just do the first day of the c25k schedule. I got up the next morning and despite my reluctance, I repeated to myself that I'd just do the first morning. I laced up and, despite the inner protestations of my mind, off I went.

Couch to 5k is such a wonderful programme. It starts so slowly, and the running sections are short, but I was so happy with myself over completing them that I found myself filled with confidence. Look at me–I'm running! Except of course, there was no one to see me, as I was plodding around at 6am in the morning and there was no one else out. But I got into the habit of jogging three times a week and each completed stage fed into the next one.

I did miss the odd run, but I generally kept going. I realised quite early that the Tokyo Olympics would be sadly out of reach, but I persevered in the early mornings, puffing and panting my way around the town, tootling along at my own speed to protect my knee. That body awareness that I had developed during yoga was helping me out here.

Summer and autumn were fine, but then I came up against the problems of winter, which seemed to exist in two types of weather–rain and heavy rain. Combined with the wind and the cold, it became impossible to get out of bed in the morning. I feared my running career was coming to an early end.

So, I set about making things a bit easier. I bought a few layers. I had my gear ready to put on as soon as I awoke. I had a raincoat hanging up if I needed it. My trainers were right beside the door. I had all the preparation done. I was making sure that I wasn't going to give myself any needless excuses to avoid having to go out in the morning–farting around in the dark and cold as you search for gear to put on is the perfect one.

The other thing I had to prepare for was my own mind. I practise a lot of meditation, and one of the things that you notice is that you have no control over thoughts. They just arise and fall away, and at the same time, you are not your thoughts. They're just like sounds or bodily sensations. You can just notice them and let them go.

So as soon as I'd wake up, I'd hear:

'It's too cold and it's raining–why don't you go out tomorrow instead?'

'Okay', I said. 'Sure, I'll put on my gear anyway and can change my mind before I leave.'

'You've already completed a run this week. Take it easy, maybe do an extra run next week?'

'OK', I said, as I put on my raincoat, hat and gloves. 'Sure, I'll just run a little bit.'

'Listen to that wind and rain. This is madness!'

'OK', I said as I laced up my boots, 'I won't go too far.'

'Go back to bed! Imagine being back under the covers. You're going to be so wet and cold. This is crazy. Stop!'

'Okay sure, I won't go far,' I said as I plodded my way through the wind and the rain and the darkness of a winter morning.

We are not our thoughts, and we don't have control over them. I was aware of them, and I acknowledged them, but ignored them. I began to notice my brain was telling me not to run, even as I was running! My motivation to make a change was the force that got me out of bed. Sure, it wasn't easy to begin with, but I kept going, because I also turned my running into a habit.

I also learned how to compromise with the critical thinking part of my brain, something we'll return to at the end of the chapter. My brain would cry 'Oh, it's much too cold and wet.' Ok, I'd say. 'Sure, we'll just go to the end of the road.' Once we got there, and the complaining started again, I'd say: 'Ok, just to the next streetlamp and then we'll turn.' And on it continued. I was compromising by suggesting little goals. Very often, I didn't run as much as I would have liked to, but I did get out and do something.

What generally happened was that once I got started and settled into a rhythm of running, my critical mind would fall away. It hadn't succeeded because I had shown that it wasn't in charge. My focus changed to ensuring that I was breathing properly, and putting one foot in front of the other. And I focused on my rewards. Firstly, there was the hot shower to come (is there anything more pleasurable than getting into the shower after a run in the cold rain?). The next reward, which took a bit longer, was climbing onto the scales. Little by little, the weight began to drop off.

And lastly, but most importantly–I had learned a new behaviour, running–by just doing it. I had overcome all my doubts, and just got out there. I got a great endorphin boost, but also a deeper satisfaction that I was in charge, and that I could make positive changes to my wellbeing. This gave me great confidence and was a great lift throughout lockdown.

When I'm doing my yoga poses, it often happens that my critical brain is still going. I can find myself in a downward dog thinking about something my boss said to me the day before and how annoying it was. I acknowledge this, and return to my breathing, inhaling and exhaling. The thought will soon dissipate before another one comes along at another stage. That's okay. Rinse and repeat. You'll find that the deeper you proceed with your practice, you're much more able to focus on your breathing and feel the stretch in your muscles.

HABIT FORMING

I remember reading years ago that if you did something for thirty days in a row, it would become a habit. However, looking into the research surrounding this, it seems some studies suggest it takes a bit longer, such as this one from the European Journal of Social Psychology[1] , which suggests that it takes 66 days on average. I have to say that hasn't been the case for me, but we all have different personalities and motivations. What I know is that as in the example of running above, repeating the same tasks daily can quickly become a habit.

Let's return to yoga again, as that's why we're here, right? It hasn't always been the case that I practice on a daily basis. I can slip into old ways and suddenly find I've gone a few weeks without hitting the mat. Life gets in the way, yadda yadda. It happens more often than I like but I don't beat myself up about it.

However, once I become aware of this (my body usually lets me know) I set about changing my behaviours. There are a few things that I do to help myself and I'm going to share them with you now.

In his bestselling book 'Atomic Habits', James Clear suggests that the best way to establish a new habit is to link it into an existing one. As detailed in my old running regime, preparation is key, and the night before I had already rolled my mat out. My yoga shorts and T-shirt are beside my bed, ready for me to put on.

Before I hit the mat, I do one more thing–I start my coffee machine. I ground the beans, fill up the water tank and place the carafe on the hob. I'm not really a fully functioning human being in the morning until I've had my coffee, but by doing this I know my coffee will be ready and waiting for me–after I've done my yoga.

And this is the important bit–my reward, for completing my short morning yoga session, is a cup of wonderful hot joe. I can hear the machine sizzling, crackling and dripping as I'm moving through my poses. Sometimes it's a short session, sometimes I'm feeling a bit tight–my body usually lets me know what I need–but all the time I know that coffee will be ready for me. This is called 'habit stacking'–stacking a new habit on top of an already existing behaviour.

The only problem for me is that as soon as I smell coffee I drop down to the floor and do a downward dog. It's not usually a problem but a few baristas have asked that I stop doing it, as they're afraid I'll injure myself and it's putting their customers off their coffee.

No, being serious again–what morning habits can you align with your gentle yoga in the mornings? Yoga before a shower? Before you turn on the radio or open the newspaper?

And it doesn't have to be in the mornings–that's just what suits me. Have a think about the rest of your day, could you fit it in before your favourite TV programme starts, or before you start to make a meal? I'm sure there's something in your day that's a daily habit. Grab a pen and start jotting down your daily routine. You'll find something in your day that you can work with. Even if it sounds like too much, perhaps there's two TV programmes that you like that run one after the other. I'm sure there's a commercial break–you can practice for a few minutes then.

What's that? Your pens in the other room? No excuses, and remember that even Newton got off the couch.

MOTIVATION

By now this book should have given you all the motivation that you need. Still, you can always remind yourself of some of the benefits of yoga–becoming more youthful and vital as you get older, living independently, helping with mood, disease etc, etc.

Let's talk for a moment about something called negativity bias.[2] This is the tendency that humans have, to focus more on the negative things around us. We've all experienced this–say you've had a work performance review, and rather than focus on all of the positive things your line manager has said, you'll isolate and dwell on the one thing they thought you could improve upon.

It's also evident when you're out with friends, and you've had a great evening with lots of conversation and laughter, but at one stage, one of your friends made a remark about something that happened in the past that caused you some embarrassment at the time. When you get home and your partner asks how your evening was, it's this that you'll most likely relay rather than the rest of the evening, which was fun.

Like many human behavioural traits, the reasons behind our tendency for negativity bias tend to be evolutionary. When we were hunter gatherers and were looking for somewhere to camp for the night, rather than focus on the abundance of firewood close by and nice view of the savannah, it was important to focus on the possibility of getting ambushed by a sabre-toothed tiger during the night. Paying attention to danger was a matter of survival.

Of course, we don't have to worry about sabre-toothed tigers so much these days, but we can still become trapped in the whirling vortex of negative thinking. There are, thankfully, some ways we can go to counter this.

Perhaps you're thinking: 'I really don't feel like doing yoga today because I'm tired.' One of the best ways of countering that is to think instead of something positive. So, you could respond with: 'I got so much energy from my yoga practice yesterday.' One that always works for me, as I relayed in my example about jogging above, is I'll say to myself: 'Sure, let's compromise. I won't do a full session; instead, I'll just do a couple of minutes.' This act of rephrasing seems to satisfy the critical part of my brain. I find that after those few minutes, because my yoga is such an ingrained habit (wake up and smell the coffee), I automatically move past those few minutes. I think this is because even though my brain is still stuck in inertia, my body enjoys it.

I think we've talked a lot about motivation and habit forming and hopefully you've learned some tips and tricks here that will get you off the couch and moving. If this is your first time to attempt yoga, fair play to you. It's not always easy to start something new. Remember that a little at a time is OK and something is always better than nothing. Be gentle with yourself and have good intentions and you'll get there.

Time for another pose? Good. This one is called the upwards hands pose and we're going to begin by doing it in the chair. Again, this is a great pose for the office or at home, suitable for any time of the day. Maybe you're sitting on a bus and need a stretch, or waiting for the traffic lights to change in your car. Again, it may seem deceptively simple, but it's great for waking up the shoulders and back muscles and helping to ease any tightness. Raising our arms in the air is generally not something that we tend to do a lot of on a daily basis, so this is really good for improving the motion in this part of the body. It also works as a gentle heart opener, really helping us mentally and physically.

SEATED ARMS OVERHEAD POSE

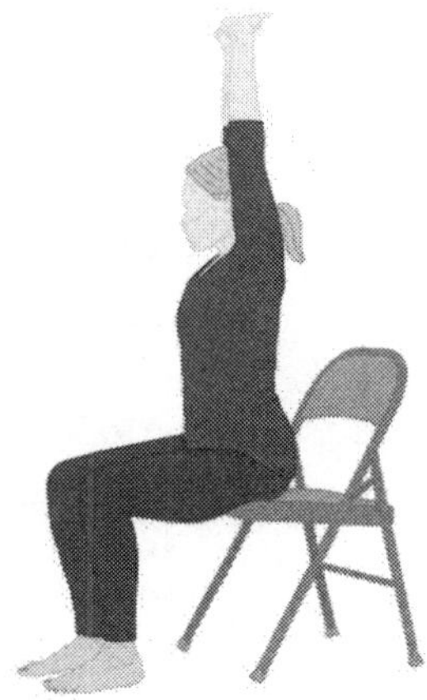

1. As usual, take your place on the chair, feet flat on the ground and arms gently by your side.
2. Keep your shoulders relaxed and let your rib cage rest naturally above your hips. Anchor your sitting bones in the chair.
3. Inhaling, raise your hands toward the ceiling and if able, interlink your fingers.
4. Push your palms towards the ceiling, exhaling.
5. Keep the shoulders relaxed, and relax your gaze, looking straight ahead.
6. Breathe in and out three times before returning your hands alongside your body to your neutral position again.

STANDING ARMS OVERHEAD POSE

If you're able to, you can do the same pose on the mat. This is a great pose for strengthening the legs, improves the posture, and is one of my go-to poses when I've just gotten out of bed as it's a full body stretch. It's also really good for breathing as it opens up the chest and allows you to breathe deeply. It helps to stimulate the nervous system and I often feel calmness descending when I'm doing this pose. As you're also stretching the body, it's great for the digestive system and it also helps with circulation in the upper body.

If you have a shoulder or neck injury, don't do this pose.

1. Take up the mountain pose which we introduced in Chapter 2. Stand tall with your feet hip width apart.
2. Inhale and bring your arms out to the sides and up above your head.
3. Bring your palms together or keep them parallel hip width apart, but just keep your shoulders relaxed and not hunched. It's automatic to pull them towards your ears–let them relax.
4. Keep rooted to your feet and try to pull your navel towards your spine. Don't have the knees too straight, keeping a slight microbend in the knees is safer.
5. You can raise your head to look towards the ceiling, but don't do this if you suffer from neck issues.
6. Exhale, return your palms to your side, and take up your mountain pose again. Repeat three times, not forgetting to breathe deeply.

6

WHY WE MIGHT NOT BE BREATHING CORRECTLY & HOW YOGA CAN HELP WHEN THE GOING GETS TOUGH

One of the most important ways in which yoga has helped me has been with my mental health, and I think it deserves a chapter of its own to look at this in a bit more detail.

This survey[1] from Mental health UK highlights the scale of the problem. A survey of over 4000 adults in 2018 (and this was before the pandemic and the current cost of living crisis) found that nearly three-quarters of those taking part, 74% in the previous year, had felt so stressed that they were unable to cope or were completely overwhelmed. That's a frightening statistic and shows the scale of the problem.

We all have good days and bad days, and even though things may be okay at the minute, the practice of an exercise like yoga helps strengthen our coping mechanisms for those times when we may need to call upon them. Yoga is another part of that armoury.

During our normal day-to-day life, we generally don't get the opportunity to practise deep breathing. Most of us take shallow gulps into the upper chests, barely allowing our breath to reach the lower belly.

And at times of stress during the day, we can also find ourselves holding the breath, which just adds to our anxiety levels.

Learning to breathe properly was one of the first things I learned to do in yoga. It may sound silly or obvious, but I had been breathing largely through my mouth and only using the upper part of my chest. Allowing the breath to come from deep and flow into the rest of my body was a game changer for me in terms of helping with my anxiety levels.

Let's try this exercise.

Take a deep breath and notice whether or not your stomach inflates or deflates. If you're anything like I used to be, it's your stomach that you suck in and then push out when you're exhaling, but it really should be the other way around. And yes, I am aware that some of us like to suck our stomachs in for good reason! But what you need to be doing in order to breathe properly is fill your body with air, expanding it, so that it contracts when you breathe out.

Whilst we're practising with the breath, here's another exercise that introduces you to the power of deep breathing.

Inhale through the nose to the count of four.

Breathe out whilst counting to four.

How did you find that? As discussed above, make sure to fill your abdomen with air as you inhale. Then, relax and contract the belly.

Is it necessary to breathe in through the nose? Ideally, yes. The nose is a natural air filter, protecting you against all the foreign particles floating about and naturally warming or cooling the air in the lungs. I should say that it is very satisfying to let out a big sigh when you are leaving a pose in some yoga moves, and there's a great pose called the 'Lions Breath' which does this, and I'll include it at the end of this chapter.

This is also a good time to advise to be careful in yoga when it comes to holding your breath for too long, as it can increase your blood pressure and result in headaches or worse, passing out. If at any time you feel faint or lightheaded, it's time to stop. Check with your clinician if this is a problem but in terms of gentle yoga, just be mindful of your breathing as it's central to your yoga practice.

STRESS-RELIEVING BREATHING

We've all heard of the 'fight or flight' response, which is when our sympathetic nervous system triggers the stress response in our body, prompting us to fight or flee. Again, this was very useful back in the days when we were worried about the old sabre-toothed tiger leaping out on us whilst we were sitting around the campfire, but less useful when thinking about something stressful that's going to be happening at work tomorrow. Living in this heightened state of alertness is extremely damaging to our physical and mental health. When faced with a situation that makes us anxious or distressed, we tend to breathe more shallowly, which doesn't help us feel any better.

It's no wonder that one of the great antidotes to stress is to practice deep breathing, as practiced by yogis over the centuries. There must be something to it! Deep breathing allows oxygen to reach all the cells in the body, harnessing energy to perform vital functions, including removing waste material, such as carbon dioxide.

Nose breathing is much more relaxing and useful than mouth breathing in these circumstances because the air is reaching the lower lobes of your lungs, thus stimulating your parasympathetic nervous system, which helps with relaxation.

Here's a simple exercise that has also helped me during times of heightened anxiety or stress. It's called alternate nostril breathing.

ALTERNATE NOSTRIL BREATHING

1. Take a seated position, whether in a chair or on the mat. Sit tall but relaxed.
2. Place your left hand on your left knee.
3. Raise your right hand to your forehead, and place your index and middle finger to rest between your eyebrows.
4. Take a good deep, cleansing breath in and out through your nose.
5. Place your right thumb over your right nostril and inhale deeply and slowly through your left nostril.
6. Close the left nostril with your middle finger and pause briefly with both nostrils closed at the top of the breath.
7. Release the thumb and start to exhale through the right nostril, pausing briefly at the end of the exhale.
8. Inhale through the right nostril, and again, at the top of the inhale, close both nostrils with the index and thumb for a brief pause. That's one complete cycle.
9. Begin the next cycle; this time open the left nostril and exhale slowly with a pause at the bottom.
10. I think it's best to repeat this five to ten times to get the benefits from it. It really helps when your heart is beating fast or your breathing feels out of control.

THE POWER AND IMPORTANCE OF BREATH

In other forms of exercise, the aim is to be completely exhausted at the end of your workout. That's fair enough, but it's certainly not the aim of yoga. Instead, the idea is that you feel calm and centred, a bit more energised, and the breath plays a big part in this.

When you're moving through poses, it becomes easy to lose touch with the breath. Maybe we're thinking about what we're going to have for our tea that evening, or something that happened in our favourite TV programme last night is on our mind. That's okay–wandering is the natural state of the mind. But the good thing is that the more you notice this in yoga, the more opportunity you have to bring the attention back to the breath.

Breathing is central to yoga. In Sanskrit, the word *pranayama* means breathing exercises and the breath is believed to help clear any emotional obstacles within us, freeing up what is called the life force, called *prana*.

I don't mind admitting that yoga has brought me to tears many times, and I know from being in classes and talking to other people, that this is something that regularly happens. I think a lot of stress and trauma is stored in the body and there is something about these poses and breathing into them that seems to unblock something. I'm sorry that I can't be more scientific than that.

I know myself that I store a lot of nervous tension in my body, and yoga is my way of releasing this. For me, it felt like the prana, the life force, is moving through my body, reinvigorating parts that were previously blocked. A shower of rain on a patch of desert, so to speak.

Feel where the emotions are, breathe into them. Let it come, let it be and let it go.

In our daily lives we suppress a lot of emotions. Yoga comes from the Sanskrit word *yuj* which means to join together, or union. Obviously, there is a union between the body and the breath but for me another union which takes place is the joining of separate parts of ourselves. It allows healing to take place.

BODY AWARENESS AND MINDFULNESS

Yoga involves listening to your body. When you start doing poses, you'll become aware when you're forcing a pose and it doesn't feel right. It's important to pay attention to these cues, make relevant adjustments and do what you feel comfortable with. Consider that yoga is an act of self-love because you are listening to the needs of your own body–you are feeling your way into a stretch, all the time breathing and adjusting your balance to what feels comfortable. This is your safe place and over time it helps us tune into our bodies again.

Mindfulness has been a bit of a buzzword for some time now and though a lot has been written about it, the simple meaning of it is: whatever you are doing, be aware of it. Its benefits include reducing anxiety, and depression, improving concentration, increasing empathy and reducing stress.

We live in a world of constant distractions, with constant demands on our time. Even if we're watching our favourite TV programme, our phone is never too far from our hands. Our attention is constantly divided. Scroll the internet, jumping between pages, with twenty-two different tabs open, to give you an idea of how frazzled your brain is, never mind our posture and our breathing.

A simple way of returning to the moment is to use that most ancient of tools, the breath. It's the first thing we did when we came into the world, and the last thing we'll take on the way out. In the words of the great spiritual teacher Thich Nhat Hanh:

Breathing in, I know I am breathing in.

Breathing out, I know I am breathing out.

In essence, that is the practice of mindfulness.

You can be present whilst washing the dishes, taking the dog for a walk, or walking along the supermarket aisles–opportunities to be present, in the here and now, are available throughout your day.

Your daily yoga practice offers you a great opportunity to be present. With the TV off, and the phone out of reach, this is your time. As you stretch, be present with that part of your body, inhaling and exhaling into and the different parts. Be aware of your body and listen if it's telling you that it's feeling pain. Feel how tight some parts of your body are and experience how a deep stretch helps. Don't worry about bending your body to get into a certain pose–the important thing is to do what you can do and be in the here and now.

Yoga is a great grounding process. The poses help you feel balanced, solid and strong, and using the breath, become rooted mentally and physically.

THE LION'S BREATH

I haven't forgotten that I said we'd do a lion's breath at the end of this chapter. It's one of my favourites because it relaxes the face and throat, engages the lungs, and just generally feels like you are releasing pent-up emotions. Let's get right into it.

1. Take a seat or sit cross-legged on your mat–whatever is most comfortable.
2. Sit upright and comfortable, hands resting in your lap and fingers spread apart.
3. Take a deep inhale of breath.
4. Open your mouth, sticking your tongue out down towards your chin.
5. Exhale with force, pushing the breath out, making a 'ha' sound as you do so. Really let it come from deep.
6. Return to a normal breathing rhythm before doing the lion's breath again. I like to do it towards the end of my practice, but you can do it at any time of the day. Feel free to do it whilst queuing to pay for your groceries. Just be careful not to scare any small children in the vicinity.

7

IS YOGA GOING TO MAKE MY EXISTING CONDITION WORSE?

In this chapter, we're going to talk a little about warming up before we move onto some poses. Preparation is key to avoiding injury before you do any exercise, so this is quite an important section.

WARMING UP

Throughout this book, we have emphasised gentle yoga, which means that you won't need to perform a vigorous warm-up schedule just to do the poses. In fact, many of the poses would be considered warm-up exercises if you were doing a vinyasa flow, which is when you move between poses seamlessly, using your breath. I can highly recommend vinyasa flows if you find that you're enjoying the poses so much that you want to extend your practice. But that's not what we're about with this book.

However, it is considered good practice to warm up and a few gentle stretches are good preparation to warm up your muscles and prepare your joints for an extended workout. Warming up helps restore your muscles' elasticity and achieve greater mobility by improving your blood circulation.

The time of day is important when it comes to warming up and exercising. I'm very much an early bird and usually rise at 6am the whole year round. For years I tried to fight this but now I accept it–it's just how my body works.

Everyone is different–some of us warm-blooded, others cold-blooded. We all know our own bodies, so you choose the best time for your workout. Maybe adjust the heating to help in the colder months to get you going.

In the winter months, when I arise, I'm usually cold and stiff. I'm able to generate a bit of heat by doing a few cat-cows or moving from a couple of downwards dogs to a plank pose. As explained in the chapter of habit forming, my mat is already rolled out, so I perform a few gentle yoga poses just to get things moving again.

I mentioned earlier that I occasionally do a bit of light jogging, and it's worth pointing out that I always perform yoga poses that involve hamstring stretches before setting out.

It's important to be careful when your muscles are cold because a run could cause a strain or a tear. I practice a few simple warm-up poses to prevent this–the old reliable downward dog and the aptly named runner's lunge. I should add that I have never picked up a hamstring or calf injury whilst running, so I think it's been working.

In the summer months when the temperature rises, I often find that I leave my yoga to the evening when the temperature has dropped and it's a bit cooler. I don't usually have any problems then as my body is properly warmed up. I try not to exercise too close to bedtime though, as when you increase your heart rate too much it can be difficult to fall asleep.

Muscles shorten and become tight when they haven't been used in a while. When they're like this, it's easy to tear and strain muscles, and develop problems with the alignment of your spine.

When stretching in yoga, don't go beyond what is comfortable. You will know when you have stretched as far as you can go, so don't push past this as it will only create injury. The great thing about yoga is that you will notice that the more you practice, the more you will be able to stretch. When I started, I couldn't touch my toes. By loosening my hamstrings over weeks of practice, I soon became able to do so. You'll be surprised at the improvements you can make to your own mobility, vital gains all the more important as we get older.

We've actually already introduced a couple of warm-up poses as we've gone through the book, but we'll mention them again at the start of the next chapter.

SHARP PAIN

We're all familiar with different types of pain. There's the pain that comes from stubbing your toe on the corner of the table. Painful, sure, but we know it's going to pass.

Then there's the other pain–sharp, stabbing, and completely out of the blue. There's pain that spreads, pain that results in swelling, pain that comes from a painful popping. When I tore the ligaments in my knee, it was like someone twisting bubble wrap. Not good. When this happens, it's a good idea to contact your doctor.

If you have been sedentary for some time and are now starting to get moving again, firstly well done, and secondly, it's natural to feel a few aches and a bit of stiffness, especially if you are exercising muscles that aren't used to it. The medical term for what you might experience the following day is 'delayed onset muscle soreness' and believe it or not, it's actually a good sign. The muscles are working and are now building more tissue to get stronger.

On the other hand, when your muscles stop feeling sore, it doesn't mean the exercises are no longer working. It just means your muscles are getting used to it. Forget about the 'no pain no grain' adage–these exercises may be moderate but they do work. Trust me, I have seen the results myself and in others.

I don't want to sound like a broken record, but look for the signs from your body that something might be wrong. This may take the form of the aforementioned sharp pain, or it could be dizziness. We've talked about the body awareness that develops as you can practice yoga and it's incredibly important when it comes to pain. Listen to your body.

DOCTOR'S WARNING

I realise this isn't the first time I've included a warning in this book but I'm going to include it one more time, especially as we move on to more exercises in the next chapter. If you have any concerns at all about exercising, have an existing medical condition, high blood pressure, or are taking medication–please consult with your doctor before you try any of these poses. A doctor will be able to advise if you should be exercising or not.

If blood pressure is a particular concern, be advised that holding your breath can cause your blood pressure to rise suddenly, which can lead to dizziness or fainting, or worse still, passing out or a stroke. Quit exercising and check in with your doctor.

Concerned about certain weight-bearing poses on your hands or knees? It may be that certain injuries mean you can't perform certain movements and that's fine, and you shouldn't test these. Again, give your physician a call. We're only introducing a range of yoga poses here, but you should be able to find something that suits you. Alternatively, you can search for other modifications to these exercises, specific to your limitations, if we haven't already covered these.

Suppose you have any doubts about your ability to do yoga without injuring yourself. In that case, it's advisable to attend a yoga class, if at all possible, as a trained yoga teacher will be able to advise better as to whether or not a pose is suitable and if it may aggravate an existing injury.

Remain aware when you are in the poses of any pain or restriction of movement. Don't push into a pose if it doesn't feel right. It's your body, you know your limits.

Most poses should be fine and not create any issues, as the emphasis is on gentle yoga. We have included modifications wherever possible, so the poses should be available to most participants.

Very often one of the statements I hear from people who don't practice yoga is that they suffer from aches and pains or have certain diseases and ailments that prevent them from doing any exercise. We are certainly all different and each of us have our own crosses to bear, but very often I feel that having certain aches and pains is in fact a sign that you *need* to exercise and bring yoga into your life. We're going to look at the role that yoga can play in helping with a range of conditions. Feel free to skip to the part relevant to you, or head over to the end of the chapter for another pose. Although I must say that reading about the benefits and relief yoga can bring to people with a range of ailments makes for a good read, firstly, because it shows how far-reaching these benefits can be and secondly, you never know when you might need to know this.

OSTEOARTHRITIS

It's estimated that a staggering 500 million people worldwide, around 7% of the population, suffer from osteoarthritis.[1] With an increase in people living longer, and obesity levels continuing to increase, this figure is only going to get much greater. What if there was an exercise that could help with this, that was cheap and was an alternative to medicines. If only... Oh, wait. I think I might know of one! And we're going to back this up with research.

I should also say at this point that I appreciate osteoarthritis can be as much to do with gender, genetics and previous injuries as it is to do with lack of exercise, but what we are hoping to do with this book is to introduce you to exercises that help to keep your bones healthier for longer. And another word of caution in relation to the exercises, something that I will make no apologies for repeating throughout this book–depending on the severity of your osteoarthritis, be extra careful because bone density loss can make your spine more fragile. Take some advice or completely avoid poses such as the forward fold, or the spinal twist.

This study we already mentioned,[2] focused on twelve poses practised by 741 participants and found that yoga was a safe and effective way to both reverse bone loss in the spine and femur, as well as producing qualitative evidence that bone quality was improved.

The Academy of Medical Royal Colleges in the United Kingdom also produced an interesting report[3] that looks at the impact of exercise on a number of conditions, including osteoarthritis, which is known as a degenerative joint disease, or 'wear and tear' arthritis. But if that's the case, it's interesting that their report found that physical exercise actually improved the condition by a massive 22-83%! A huge figure, but what was just as important is that it didn't lead to a worsening of the condition.

This same report also refers to several other conditions that are affected positively by exercise, and I think they're worth repeating here.

BACK PAIN

I mentioned my friends before who played golf and suffered back pain. They could have decided that they couldn't play golf anymore and taken up the popular sport of seeing 'how many pints you can drink in one night' and felt a bit sorry for themselves. They would have been giving up something they enjoyed, as well as the mental benefits that come from being with friends and socialising.

Instead, they set about finding out what they could do about back pain–discovered yoga, and never looked back. They do still drink pints, and there is the odd complaint about the odd ache and pain–but they are still golfing and hope to do so until they reach a ripe old age. As they're fond of saying to me, golf carts are a great invention and will be there when they need them.

Speaking of which, just look at this study from the Harvard Medical School.[4] It refers to a study of 313 people with chronic back pain and found that a weekly yoga class helped with chronic back pain more so than standard treatment for the condition. A meta-analysis of a further 17 studies, with 1600 participants, found that yoga helped people in their day to day living with conditions such as fibromyalgia, osteoporosis, and curvature of the spine. I should have put the researchers in touch with my golf buddies as well.

So, it seems that yoga works well for back pain because it gently strengthens the muscles in the back and helps with upright posture and movement. Another important point about yoga is the focus that it places on stretching. Our muscles carry a lot of stress, and by stretching and releasing these muscles, we can relieve a lot of the tension. A lot of this depends on how long we can hold the pose, whilst also breathing in and out of that part of the body. Keep in mind that your ability to hold a pose improves over time.

Everything is interconnected. Let's consider the hamstrings for a moment. If you stretch these it helps with the range of motion in the pelvic area, thus leading to a reduction of stress in the lower back. Also, bear in mind that when you stretch in yoga, it improves your blood flow and circulation. This allows nutrients to flow in, and toxins to flow out, helping to nourish the muscles and soft tissue in the lower back.

Yoga can also help with disc issues by building core strength and flexibility in the spine, but again, be careful with the forward folds or any pose that causes the spine to curve.

One of the questions that medical practitioners and physios will often ask you when you say you have back pain is: "Have you thought about strengthening your core?" This is great advice, as when you build up the muscles in your back, trunk, abdomen, hips and legs, you make sure that your spine is better supported. The great news here is that yoga is a super exercise for strengthening your core. Anyone who has even done a plank, chair or boat pose can certainly attest to that.

DEMENTIA

The previously mentioned AOMRC study (see footnote 21) makes the significant connection between physical activity and improved cognition in patients with early signs of Alzheimer's disease, and studies have consistently shown that exercise can reverse brain atrophy.

I also found this research, carried out by the Florida Atlantic University particularly interesting.[5] Looking at patients who took two 45-minute classes per week for 12 weeks, it found the participants fully engaged with each of the sessions and that it led to an improvement in their quality of life as well as helping with depression and balance, something that's really important the older that you get.

There's been so much research into the links between exercise and improvements in cognitive processes that it would be impossible to list them all here. But if I may include this one[6] from the National Library of Medicine, which examined the use of yoga in old people's homes and found that participants showed significant improvement in verbal and visual memory, attention and working memory, verbal fluency and processing speed.

I think what this research shows is that our brains are perhaps a bit more flexible and adaptable than scientists have previously thought. Yoga can play a major role as a form of exercise that helps to prevent what has been seen before as an inevitable decline in a condition that the World Health Organisation estimates will affect 78 million people worldwide by 2030.

I think the importance of the role that yoga can play in the treatment of dementia can't be underestimated. Improving circulation and enabling the body to engage in a range of motions can help with falls, particularly affecting older sufferers. It also helps with body awareness, allowing patients to understand their own limitations.

LIGAMENT TEARS

As previously mentioned in the introduction, this is something I have first-hand experience of and one of the reasons I got interested in yoga in the first place. Although I damaged the ligaments in my knee, it's just as easy to do them in the shoulders, hips and ankles, especially as we accumulate wear and tear over the years.

Yoga is great for strengthening the muscles around these joints, helping to protect them. When I do a lunge in my warrior pose, I am strengthening my glutes, hamstrings and quadriceps, and the knee.

Another thing I recall from my time recovering from knee ligament damage, was that I was still able to perform gentle yoga poses, obviously not targeting the knee but concentrating on other poses and stretches. I concentrated on poses that stretched the upper body, never placing pressure on the knee. Then, when I started to get stronger and the knee began to heal, I slowly began to try poses like the child's pose and some seated forward folds. One of the problems I encountered was worrying about the stability of the knee, and I think this can be as much of a mental as a physical problem. Strengthening the knee gave me the confidence to get moving freely again.

I should also say that I have attended classes where some of the students had knee or hip replacements, with some adaptations of course, and were able to fully participate in the class.

FIBROMYALGIA AND FATIGUE

Yoga has been long recommended as a form of aerobic exercise to help with fibromyalgia as it helps with both physical function and improving a person's sense of wellbeing. Gentle yoga is of course a good way to stretch and loosen up muscles and joints. Dizziness is also a symptom of fibromyalgia, so seated postures or those practised on the ground are to be recommended. As seen throughout this book, a lot of yoga emphasises breathing, so you're not just rushing willy-nilly from pose to pose–you are taking your time, breathing in and out, helping you to relax and stay calm. At this stage, you know I love my research so this study[7] showed that yoga helps with sleep, increased muscle strength and improved mobility and flexibility, pain management and leads to an increase in wellbeing.

DEPRESSION

The link between depression and exercise is a well-established one–research in this report[8] suggests there is a 20% and 33% lower chance of developing depression in adults who participate in daily physical activity. This report[9] found that symptoms of depression could be reduced in patients practising yoga because it reduced cortisol levels, thus helping with stress and anxiety. Again, as mentioned previously, breathing plays a big part in reducing anxiety and introducing feelings of relaxation, helping to keep cortisol levels down.

I think another way that yoga can help with depression is that when people are suffering from low mood, they really don't feel like leaving the house. They often can't find the motivation to attempt even simple tasks, so the idea of joining a gym or a class can terrify them. It's easy to get trapped in a spiral of low mood and poor self-esteem, and doing even the smallest tasks can seem like scaling Mount Everest.

I would say here that the beauty of performing gentle yoga at home allows you to start your own exercise programme, going at your own speed. Maybe you only do one exercise at a time–that's okay. You're building up your confidence, and hopefully once you begin to feel the benefits, you'll be encouraged to do more. And maybe once you start to feel better, you might want to join a yoga class, and this is a great way to meet people. Humans aren't meant to spend so much time alone, and as the lockdown during the pandemic showed, we are social creatures. Being around people can help to alleviate depression and improve your mood.

I think there's also a great boost to be had by learning something new. It's easy to get stuck in a routine and learning a new type of exercise is a great way of doing something completely new. It can contribute greatly to improving our physical, physiological and emotional well-being. It's not competitive, although as you progress your practice deepens, you become more flexible and you can always try new poses. Most importantly, it's fun.

Something else I would like to say about classes here is that I find them a safe, non-judgemental space. I have generally found that you don't have the same results-driven environment that you find in gyms, and you just do the poses at your own pace, knowing your own limitations. For me, yoga classes have always been a warm and welcoming place.

HEART DISEASE

Moderate exercise has been shown to lead to marked improvements in cardiovascular health. This review[10] of clinical research found that yoga had a significant impact on cardiometabolic risk factors, helping to reduce both cholesterol and blood pressure. Those who suffered from heart disease found both lower heart and blood pressure rates, whilst also enjoying a boost in their mental health scores.

A lot of the restorative benefits of yoga come from deep breathing, which allows us to bring more oxygen into the body, and combined with stretching, allows us to feel more relaxed and centred. It's no wonder that it helps with blood pressure and cortisol levels.

Again, one of the important factors in the type of yoga we are advocating in this book is that it is gentle and restorative. It's important to remember that if you have high blood pressure or are suffering from heart disease, you need to focus on exercises that don't place the head below the heart. Standing up too quickly, or moving with speed from a seated pose into a standing pose, is not recommended.

OBESITY

Exercise really only has a moderate effect in reducing obesity.[11] Thirty minutes of aerobic activity is recommended at least five times a week if you want to see any change in your weight, but you really need to combine it with dietary measures if you want to see any major changes. There's no point in running to the chip shop, and one piece of advice that I always think is worth remembering is that 'You can't outrun a fork.' Never a truer word has been spoken.

But even if you aren't losing weight, it's important to remember that there are other benefits, as we have highlighted throughout this chapter. From reducing the risk of type 2 diabetes, to helping with cardiovascular disease, there should be plenty of motivation for engaging with an exercise programme.

With reference to yoga, one of the best ways it can help is to tackle some of the problems associated with obesity, as this study shows.[12] One of the issues with putting on weight is that you find it harder to motivate yourself and it becomes difficult to get off the couch and anxiety and depression develop as a result. Gentle yoga is a great way of taking small steps to get moving again, to allow you to develop some confidence. And if you can't get to a class, or maybe feel a bit self-conscious in front of others, you can practice some yoga moves in the comfort of your own living room. Just be conscious of other health complications that you may have and don't put too much pressure on yourself and remember that we all have to start somewhere.

In the study mentioned just above, the results showed that yoga played a part in helping with mood and improving a sense of well-being. High levels of cortisol are also shown to be present in people with depression, and yoga plays an important part in helping to reduce this.

If you are reading this and suffer from weight problems, I think when it comes to yoga, the most important part is showing up and getting on the mat or the chair. Fair play to you for recognising that you want to change your body, heart and mind; gentle yoga is a great place to begin that journey.

If you go to classes, don't compare yourself to others. We all have to start somewhere and like Quality Street chocolates, we come in a variety of shapes and sizes. Keep returning to your breath and continue to feel the awareness of your body. Blocks are a great help if you go to classes, as they bring the ground close to you. Keep a towel close by for sweating. If you have wrist problems, wear some strapping. Don't push your body into poses that you can't do, and modify them where you can.

Be gentle and kind to yourself and know that with practice and patience, change will come. As the saying goes, the first step is the hardest, and by doing these exercises you will have taken it. Well done and keep going.

NERVE PAIN

Nerve pain can be a familiar problem for many people–tingling, numbness, cramping, and weakness can occur across a wide range of diseases and are a common side effect of many. The good news about yoga is that the one thing that can really help with circulation is movement, and there's plenty of that in the poses. And another useful point to make here is that we continually refer to 'body awareness' in yoga, so as you are exploring your body in slow and safe movements, you can pay attention and see the effect that the pose is having on your body. You can see what works and doesn't work.

INSOMNIA

This is something that I have direct experience of, as I often find myself waking in the early hours with my heart racing. As anyone will tell you, we don't tend to think happy thoughts at 3.44 am.

This CDC report[13] found that a whopping 55% of yoga practitioners found that their sleep improved whilst practising, whilst 85% found that stress was reduced. The day that has just passed plays a huge part in getting a good night's sleep, although it's generally a combination of a variety of factors (I could write another book on sleep hygiene).

If you have woken and found your mind racing with anxious thoughts about the day ahead, you'll know how debilitating it can be, especially when you can't fall asleep again and spend the next day tired and cranky. Insomnia can become a crippling condition that can have a devastating impact on your day-to-day living.

Most moderate forms of exercise will help with your sleep. If I haven't practised yoga for a couple of days, I'll notice my sleep beginning to suffer. There's something about the deep breathing and stretching the muscles that brings relaxation benefits to my body.

If I'm going through a particularly stressful period in my life, I'll notice that it becomes hard just to fall asleep. Usually what I'll do here is practise a couple of gentle poses before I go to bed–nothing too aerobic, as I don't want to get my heart rate too high–more a couple of gentle spinal twists, a child's pose, a supine twist or hugging my knees into my chest. A couple of nights of these and I begin to drop off naturally again. As usual, it's about listening to my body. The more you practice yoga, the more you'll notice this great ability, called body awareness, which allows you to tune into your body.

When it comes to waking up early and not being able to drop off again, I'll practise a bit of deep breathing, really focusing on making the exhale as long as possible. Sometimes this works, sometimes it doesn't, but it usually relaxes me. If I find myself lying in bed for more than half an hour, I tend to get up and start my day, and as my yoga mat is already unrolled, I'll greet the day with a few poses.

When it comes to sleep, for me it's always been more about quality than quantity. If I oversleep, I can often feel groggy, whilst I feel much better with six hours of good sleep. When it comes to sleep, everyone's different and you'll know your own limitations.

I think that one of the things that is important to remember about the use of yoga as a treatment across a range of disease and ailments as seen above, is that it is cheap (much cheaper than medication) and that it can be practiced in the home. We'll continue to emphasise this throughout this book and will make no apologies for repeating the message. These are exercises that can bring great improvements to your health and wellbeing and you can incorporate them into your day-to-day living! How many exercise programmes can you say that about?

Alright, I think I've mentioned enough about disease and research now and hopefully you're in no doubt as to the efficacy of yoga as a form of physical therapy. So, on that note, time for another exercise.

~

CAT-COW

This is another exercise that can be done both seated and on the mat. It's particularly good for helping with neck and shoulder tensions, something that we all suffer from given that we spend so much time bent over our phones, dishes or crouched at our desks. In fact, this is one that I do regularly in my office chair. I've also done it in Zoom meetings while working from home, always making sure I had the camera turned off. Not that it's embarrassing for anyone to see you doing a cat-cow, and I personally wish my boss would do a few of them.

Although it's often seen as a warm-up pose, cat-cow also helps to relieve stress, improves the flexibility of your spine, opens up your chest to help with breathing and strengthens and stimulates your organs. There is a saying that 'you are only as young and happy as your spine' and I think that never a truer word was spoken. I love this pose because I can almost feel the energy moving up and down my spine and it's such a relief when I've been sitting too long. It's really good for back pain and shoulder stiffness, and I can feel the benefits almost immediately. I remember doing this pose during a twelve-hour leg of a flight to Australia and my body almost cried with relief.

This is also a particularly good pose for those with rheumatoid arthritis or osteoporosis and can help to reduce symptoms, especially at an early stage of the disease, however the pose needs to be modified for those with compromised bone density. Also, be careful if you have a spinal injury with this one–in fact, it's best avoided until you have taken medical advice or spoken to a physio. We will suggest a modified pose for those with osteoporosis on the next page, however, make sure to speak to your doctor before you try.

For those who are able to do this pose on the mat, take up a tabletop position. This is when you rest your hands underneath your shoulders and spread your fingers wide. Spread your weight amongst your fingers rather than on your wrists. Rest your knees under your hips, keeping them hip-width apart. Keep the tops of your feet flat on the mat and tuck your chin in slightly. Inhale.

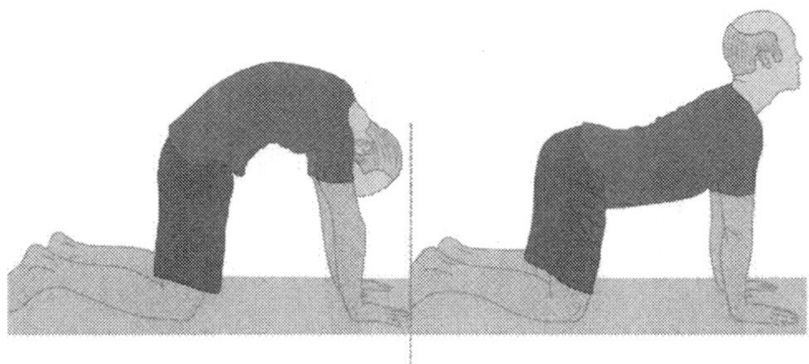

1. Exhale, drawing your belly to your spine and arching your back. Bend your head downwards but don't force your chin onto your chest. This is the cat pose.
2. Now for the cow part of the pose. Inhale, and drop your belly downward and look upwards. Draw your shoulders away from your ears.
3. Exhale, coming into your cat pose. Inhale into your cow. Repeat ten times, taking the time to stretch and breathe.

CAT-COW MODIFIED FOR OSTEOPOROSIS

Your upper back can be at a risk of fracture, therefore you should only curve your tailbone in this exercise. This helps to feel a nice stretch in the lower back, imagine a dog with its tail between its legs. With that, you're not putting the bones in your upper back in a compromised position.

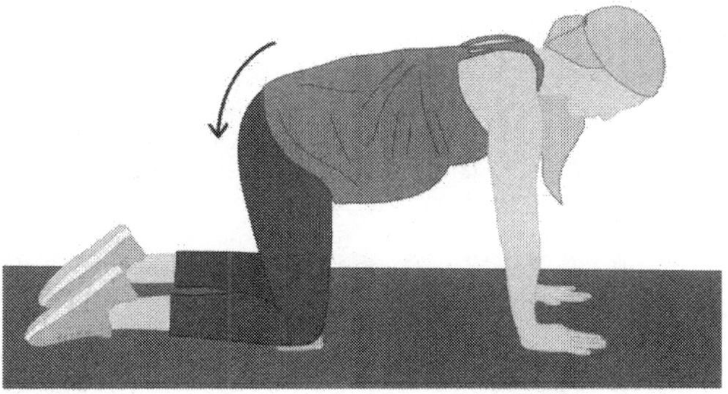

1. On the mat, take up a tabletop position as described above, but make sure your spine is straight with your head aligned with your spine naturally, eyes looking down on the mat. Your head is neither dropped down or hyperextended upwards. Take a deep breath in.
2. For the cat position, exhale and curve the tailbone slightly under, but avoid rounding your upper back or dropping your head.
3. Return your tail back up to neutral position.
4. You can safely and fully go into the cow position, dropping your belly down and looking upwards. Inhale as you're channelling your inner cow.
5. Repeat ten times, taking the time to stretch and breathe.

CAT-COW SEATED

1. Sit upright on a chair with your spine straight and your feet flat on the floor. Place your hands on your knees or the tops of your thighs, whichever feels most comfortable.
2. To do the cow pose, just like above, inhale and arch your spine, rolling your shoulders down and back.
3. On the exhale, round the spine and let the chin drop towards the chest, allowing your head and shoulders to drop forward into the cat pose.
4. Repeat ten times, inhaling on your cow pose, exhaling on the cat.

8

POSES (ALWAYS WARM UP FIRST!)

Throughout the book, we've introduced you to a few poses along the way. Hopefully you've found these enjoyable and easy to understand. We've tried to make them as simple and straightforward as possible, whilst being beneficial to your health. The majority of the poses featured have also included modifications, wherever possible.

The idea is that poses should feel comfortable, and for you not to strain to the point where you begin to experience discomfort. You can certainly push yourself to the edge of poses, but not into pain. That's certainly not the intention here. How do you feel in the pose–can you turn your attention away from your constant thoughts and just tune into your body and see how it feels?

If you have osteoarthritis, it's best to avoid any bending poses that you find here. I have mentioned that earlier, but I appreciate that not everyone reads a book in a linear fashion, jumping to the sections that interest them most.

For any of the exercises here, if you encounter a bit of tightness, see if you can focus on that area by slowing down and breathing through it.

The poses featured so far have included:

The Mountain Pose in Chapter 2

The Easy Pose and the Easy Seated Twist in Chapter 3

The Seated and Standing Side Stretch in Chapter 4

The Standing and Seated Arms Overhead Pose in Chapter 5

Deep Breathing, Alternate Nostril Breathing and Lion's Roar Breath in Chapter 6

The Cat-Cow in Chapter 7

Take a moment and remind yourself of the mountain pose from Chapter 2, either seated or standing. From this foundational position, we can practice and move into a number of other poses. We'll include some warm-up movements and gentle stretches as well.

SHOULDER ROLLS

Inhale and exhale as you roll your shoulders, clockwise, then anti-clockwise. Try this four times on each side.

SHOULDER RAISE I

This is a great one for releasing tension, as a lot of stress tends to accumulate in the shoulder region, gathering because we sit for extended periods of time, as well as down to poor posture and alignment.

1. Taking a big inhale, raise the shoulders up.

2. Hold for a breath, then sigh and exhale, letting all of that tension leave.
3. Repeat four times.

SHOULDER RAISE II

1. Another good way to do this one is to raise the right shoulder up, whilst dropping the left shoulder down towards the hips.
2. Move your right shoulder gently towards your back and downwards, as your left shoulder moves in the opposite direction, forwards and upwards.
3. Change direction after a few cycles.

NECK ROTATION

This is another excellent warm-up exercise, as it helps to reduce the stiffness and tension in the neck/shoulder/head region. This is especially good if you find yourself seated for long periods of time, and I do it quite a bit in my desk job. My boss has seen me doing this one as well, but he's OK with it–it's only when I roll my eyes at him that he gets annoyed. As I do this one, my neck makes lots of pops and noises, and I find it particularly satisfying. It goes without saying that you shouldn't do this one if you have a neck injury as the pops and crackles mightn't be just as satisfying.

Keep this one slow and easy, nice and smooth. Definitely don't be yanking your head sharply in any direction. The crown of your head should be directly over your tailbone for proper alignment. There's no need to be ramrod straight in these poses.

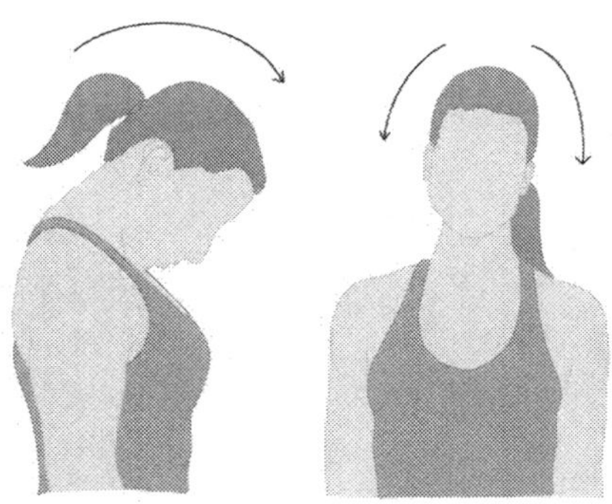

1. Inhale and relax in the shoulders and the jaw.
2. Exhale and let your head drop gently towards your chest.
3. Inhale and draw your head back to the centre again.
4. Repeat 4 times.
5. Take a deep inhale and let the head drop towards the right shoulder on the exhale.
6. Inhale and raise the head to the centre again.
7. Do the same on the other side.

8. Repeat 4 times.
9. Take a deep inhale and on the exhale let the head roll in a circle, towards your left shoulder then to the centre, chin towards the chest. When you get here, inhale as you move the head up again on the right then back to looking straight ahead.
10. Repeat four times on the left, before doing the same circles on the right.

THORACIC ROTATIONS

This is a great pose for helping with spine flexibility.

1. Lift your arms and place your hands on either side of your head.
2. Take an inhale and twist your body to the side.
3. Hold it here for a moment, before exhaling and returning to the neutral position.
4. Repeat on the other side.

DELTOIDS STRETCH

Again, this is one you can move into from your mountain pose, either sitting or standing. The deltoids are the muscles around the shoulders and upper arms and help with rotation. It keeps the muscles loose and flexible.

1. Inhale and bring your right arm across your shoulder line, and hook your left arm gently under it, pulling the right arm gently into the chest. Exhale as you feel the stretch. Repeat with the left arm.
2. Give yourself a good hug. Think of it as a reward for picking up and reading this excellent book!

Along with the side stretches and cat-cow previously mentioned in the other chapters, these are great warm-up exercises to get you started and help you loosen up. Speaking of loosening up, here's a nice easy one to get us going.

STANDING PELVIC CIRCLES

This is a nice simple movement but really helpful for the glutes, pelvic floor muscles and abdominal muscles.

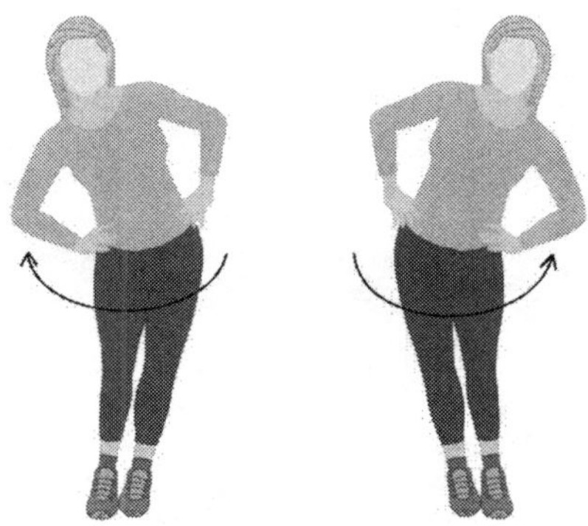

1. Stand in your mountain pose with your hands on your hips.
2. On an inhale, draw a circle with your hip as you move forward–then take an exhale as you move backwards. Do this nice and slowly, making your circle as wide as possible, moving as always with your breath.
3. Do five on each side, before moving in an anticlockwise direction.

We're going to continue with some poses for those able to take to the mat. Don't worry if you can't do these as we'll follow up with some chair poses.

TABLE TOP RAISED LEG

On the mat, take up a table top position, with your hands under your shoulders and knees under your hips. (This is also the pose you'd take up if you were doing the cat-cow.) This pose is great for building stability and strength in the core, abdomen and shoulders. It works to lengthen the spine and stretch our limbs, correcting body alignment.

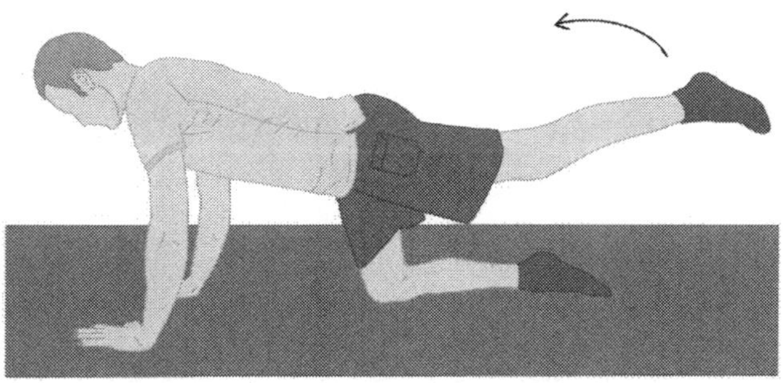

1. If you find your knees are a bit sore and stiff on the mat, feel free to put a blanket, pillow or towel underneath them to offer a bit more support.
2. Extend the right knee, keeping the toes flexed on the mat, really feeling the stretch. Use the left knee as balance, keeping the spine nice and straight, head aligned with the spine.
3. Rock back and forth a few times on the toes, breathing in and out, nice and smooth.
4. On one of those forward movements, lift the right leg, turning the bottom of the right foot up towards the sky. This is great for the core muscles, so try and lift it as high as you can, without straining and spread your weight through your fingers by clawing through them, rather than putting too much weight on your wrists.

TABLE TOP RAISED LEG IN A CHAIR ALTERNATIVE

If you are not able to go down on the mat, you can sit comfortably in your seat and combine the Seated Arms Overhead pose from Chapter 5 with a seated knee extension.

1. Seat rooted in your chair with feet firmly on the floor, raising your arms overhead.
2. Whilst your arms stay stretched out overhead, lift your right foot up and stretch your leg out in front of you.
3. Stay here for a few breaths and then lower your leg and arms back down.
4. Bring your arms back up and repeat with left leg, really enjoying the stretch and working on those core muscles.

BIRD DOG POSE

Another variation of the table top which is really good for the abdominals and back support. This is known as bird dog pose and will both challenge and improve your balance the more you practice it. This is a good exercise for your spinal erectors which are important for maintaining an upright position as we get older, to avoid the 'old folks' posture. All the while strengthening our lower back, hamstrings, glutes, arms and core in general, as well as building awareness, balance and coordination in our body.

1. Assume table top position as described above, hands under your shoulders and knees under your hips.
2. Whilst keeping your head aligned with your spine rather than tilting it upwards or down, stretch your right arm forward and left leg back.
3. Image a cup of tea resting on your back so that you stay nice and straight and draw your belly button towards your spine. Perhaps imagine this will be the cup of tea you drink as a reward when you are finished with yoga for the day.

4. After you've done it on one side (right arm forward, left back leg pointing back) repeat on the other side.
5. Repeat this pose four times.

EXTENDED CHILD'S POSE

From the bird dog pose, you can fall back into an extended child's pose to relax your muscles and stretch your spine.

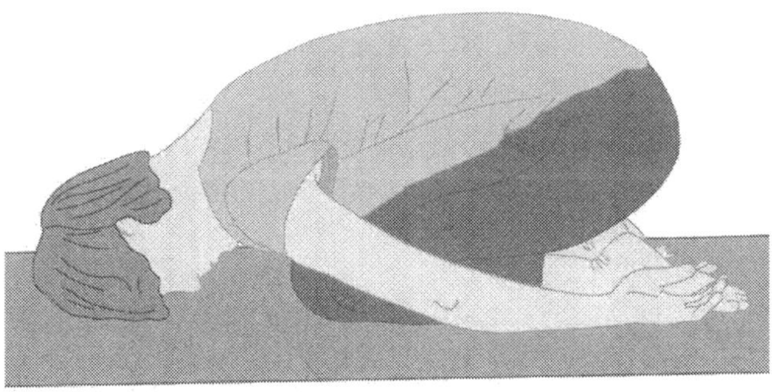

1. Touching the big toes together, keep your knees as wide as possible and lower yourself down.
2. Rest your arms straight on the floor behind you, palms up and shoulders relaxed.
3. Stay in this restorative pose for a minute, breathing all the time, before moving into the table top again.

SEATED EXTENDED CHILD'S POSE

You can also perform a child's pose from a seated position by just using another chair in front and stretching your arms over before bringing your hands to rest on the opposing chair and resting for five breaths, enjoying the stretch.

STANDING FORWARD FOLD

Don't be doing this if you suffer from osteoporosis, dizziness, vertigo, disk or spinal injuries; knee, hip, pelvis or rib injuries. You can also modify this stretch by just moving your hands down as far as the edge of the chair in front of you. Another option is a half standing fold, where you rest your hands on your thighs.

Pay attention to your reach in this pose, getting deeper each time you exhale. This is a great pose for strengthening the lower back and increasing mobility (handy for bending down in the garden to tend your plants or tie your shoelaces) but be careful with it.

1. Standing with your feet hip width apart, bend over like a rag doll, touching the floor or as far as you can fold (or rest your hands on the edge of your chair).
2. Try to breathe freely for a minute, trying to move deeper into the pose each time, before pushing into your feet and rising slowly.

SEATED FORWARD FOLD

A further modification for this pose is the seated forward fold from the chair.

1. Exhale as you let your weight hang heavy, hands to the floor if you can reach that far.
2. Take five breaths in this pose–it's great for stretching the lower back muscles.

TOE STRETCH

This requires a degree of flexibility so don't get frustrated with this pose. Practiced daily, you'll soon find your flexibility improving. With each day you should be able to see small increments.

Even if you can only reach as far as your shins, knees or thighs–that's OK. You'll still get the benefits from the stretch.

1. Sit up, legs out straight in front of you.
2. Raise your hands above with an inhale, and with the out breath reach towards your toes.
3. Bend forward from your hips.

This is a really handy stretch to see if you need to cut your toenails.

SEATED TOE STRETCH

You can do this same stretch seated on a chair. As well as stretching the hamstrings, this pose is good for the lower back and calves.

1. Sit up tall in your chair with your shoulders down and relaxed.
2. Place your feet slightly out in front of you with your hands on your knees.
3. Slide your hands down your legs to your feet or just as far you're able.
4. Hold the stretch for around thirty seconds, which you should feel in your lower back and the back of your legs.

SEATED LEG STRETCH

This is a great exercise for engaging your core muscles, allowing your back to sit nice and straight.

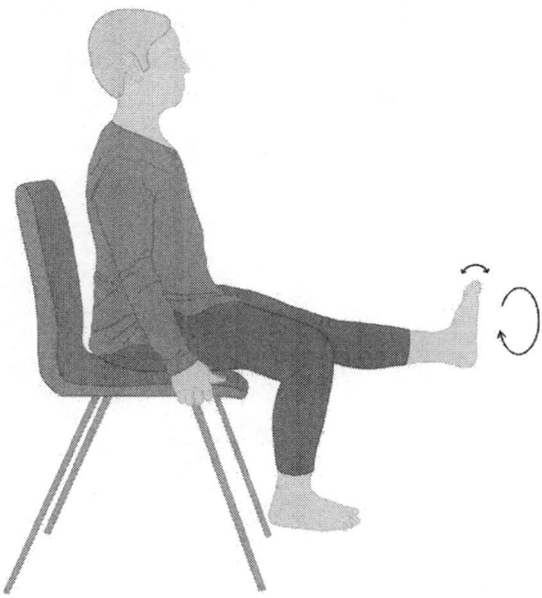

1. Sitting on your chair, hands resting on palms, nice and alert.
2. Extend your left leg, then flex and point your foot. Repeat this four times.
3. Then rotate the ankle in a circular motion for 15 seconds.
4. Repeat on the right leg.

KNEES TO CHEST POSE

Don't do this pose if you have a hernia, abdominal surgery, spinal surgery, or knee or hip injury.

This is a great pose if you are having any stomach issues–indigestions, bloating, flatulence or constipation. If you're taking part in a yoga class, just remember that there are other people around! On the rare occasions when I have overindulged with food or drink, I find this a great pose for hangovers.

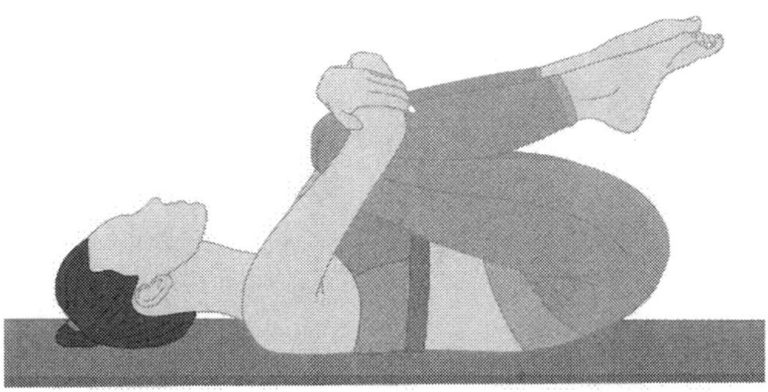

If you're doing this on the mat:

1. Lie with your back on the floor, legs and arms extended.
2. Inhale and draw your knees to your chest, clasping your arms around them.
3. Keep your back flat to the floor, shoulders and collarbone relaxed. Draw your tailbone down the mat, lengthening your spine.

4. Tuck your chin in and breathe smoothly in and out for a minute.
5. If you feel stable in this pose, rock gently backwards, forwards, or left and right for a nice little spinal massage.
6. Release out of the pose and repeat.

KNEES TO CHEST IN THE CHAIR

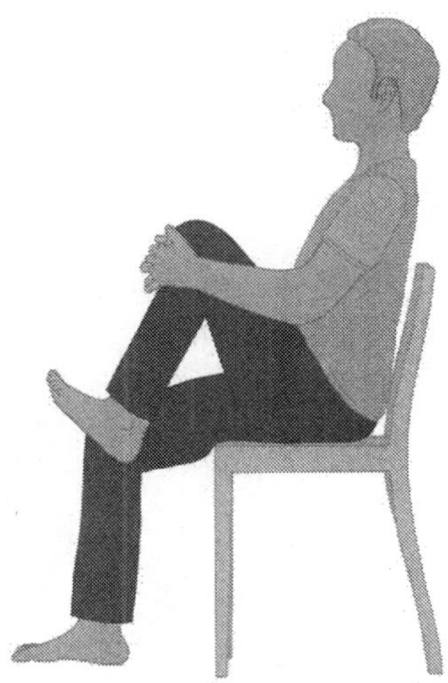

1. Seated on a chair, relaxed and straight.
2. Interlace your left fingertips around your left knee and gently raise it off the ground and up towards your chest, squeezing gently.
3. Try not to hunch your shoulders–instead root yourself down on your chair.
4. Relax and inhale and exhale for thirty seconds.
5. If you are able to, bring your left foot over to rest on top of

your right knee, but that will depend on how tight your hips are. Don't worry if you can't but if you can it's a lovely stretch.

6. Repeat on the right leg.

EAGLE ARMS POSE

This is another pose you can do either standing or seated–it's especially helpful for the shoulder joints.

1. Breathe in and extend your arms to the side.
2. Exhale and bring them back in front of you, moving the left arm under your right and reaching both hands to the shoulders, giving yourself a bit of a hug. And who doesn't need a hug now and then?
3. Inhale, and lift your arms a bit higher.
4. Exhale and let your shoulders drop.

5. Repeat five times.

REVERSE ARM HOLD

This is another pose that can be done seated or standing and is a great chest opener as well as being a fantastic stretch for the shoulders.

1. Exhale and roll the shoulders forward a little, so that your palms are facing behind you.
2. Bend your elbows and let your hands swing behind your back.
3. Clasp your hands (fingers, hand, wrists or elbows, whichever you can manage) and gently pull away from each other.
4. Hold for five breaths.
5. Repeat and reverse if the left hand was grasping the right wrist etc.

CAMEL POSE

This is a good pose for the back muscles, as well as stimulating the central nervous system. You can do this pose seated, standing or kneeling.

1. In a chair, bring your sitting bones to the chair's edge, grounding down with your feet to feel stable and balanced.
2. Place your hands on your lower back, hands pointing down. Roll your shoulders back and open your chest.
3. Hold for five breaths.

TREE POSE

This pose does require balance and coordination, but as always, we've included modifications where necessary. This is a great one for stretching and strengthening the ligaments and tendons in your feet, helps to provide stability to hips, thighs, groin and pelvis, and because you are engaging your core, helps to strengthen it too.

If you have balance issues, do this close to a wall or use your chair to rest your hand.

1. Stand next to the back of the chair, with the chair on the right-hand side of where you're standing. Place the right hand on the back of the chair.
2. Rotate the left leg away from the body, and depending on your flexibility, place the heel of the left foot above the ankle or on the calf muscle. Lift your arm overhead.
3. Repeat on the other side. When you feel your balance improving in this pose, you'll eventually feel confident enough

to try it without the chair or the wall. And it's OK to have a wobble now and then, but I always find it helps to focus on your breath or pick a spot on the wall to keep your attention on.

MODIFICATIONS FOR THE TREE POSE

If you have osteoarthritis, rest your right leg on a low chair or stool instead of your left leg. Open your right knee without turning your pelvis.

If you're still having difficulty and have used the wall and chair where needed, practice this pose by lying on the mat. And if raising your knee is too problematic for you, just keep the ball of your foot on the ground whilst resting your heel against the other side. This is such a good pose, and you'll still gain benefits whatever the modifications. It's great for building and strengthening muscles in the feet, calves, thighs, shins and knees. And as we discussed earlier, balance is something that becomes all important when we are trying to protect ourselves from falls as we get older.

We can do a variation of the tree pose in the chair that can help with balance.

1. From the mountain pose, reach for your right leg below the knee, or as low down as you can go, and raise it up as close to your chest as possible. The shoulders will naturally rise as you do this, so keep them lowered, and press your sitting bones into the chair to help you feel balanced.
2. Try to engage your core, keeping the spine straight and breathing all the time.
3. Lower the right leg and repeat the left leg.

TREE POSE (ADVANCED)

1. Stand tall in your mountain pose, arms hanging loosely by your side.
2. Move your weight to your left leg and bring your right leg up, bending it at the knee.
3. Place your right foot against the inside of your left ankle, or if you are feeling supple, move it as high up your calf as you can.
4. Keep your back straight, careful not tip too far forward. Don't push into your knee joint. If you're incredibly flexible and bendy, you could aim for the inside of your right thigh.
5. Join your palms together as if you are praying and try to raise your arms above your head. Don't forget to keep breathing.
6. Stay in this pose for thirty seconds, recalibrating each time you stumble. That's okay, and this is a pose that you will notice great improvements in the more that you practice it.
7. Repeat on the other side.

This is one of those classical poses that if anyone sees you, they'll think wow, that person really knows their yoga!

WARRIOR 2

This all-body pose will work your groin, legs, hips and chest. A little bit more complicated but still very doable, this is a great pose for strengthening and grounding, as well as opening and lengthening. Avoid this pose if you have a hip or knee injury.

1. Stand in a wide position with your feet parallel, approximately three feet apart.
2. Extend your arms straight out from your sides. Relax your shoulders away from your ears.
3. Turn your left foot out 90 degrees, then bend your knee into a lunge. Be sure to keep your knee directly above your ankle

and pointing over your toes. Distribute the weight evenly between both legs. Turn your head to the left and look over your fingers.
4. Stay for five breaths.
5. Repeat on the right-hand side.

WARRIOR 2 IN CHAIR

Doing the pose this way helps if you have issues with balance.

1. From the edge of your seat, align your right leg so that the side of your inner thigh is parallel to the right edge of the chair.
2. Extend your left leg out to the side away from the chair. Make sure your right leg lines up with the arch of your left foot.
3. Pressing down on the floor keeps the legs activated. Pull your

navel in toward your spine, stack your vertebrae and lift your breastbone upward to open the chest.

4. Spread your arms out to the sides parallel to the floor, palms facing down.
5. Relax your shoulders and breathe five times. Repeat on the other side.

DOWNWARD DOG

The downward dog is one of the first poses people will mention when you tell someone that you are practising yoga. Although it's mostly done on the mat, with a few modifications we're going to show how it can also be done using the chair.

If you have wrist problems, refer to the next pose instead, downward dog on the wall. And don't hold it for too long if you have blood pressure issues.

This is a great energising pose, and I always try to include it in my morning routine. It's a great chest opener, helps to build strength and flexibility in the hamstrings, shoulders and arms, and is a great stretch for the back–which you would know if you own a cat or a dog.

1. From the mat, get into the table top position again–knees beneath the hips, hands shoulder width apart but slightly forward from your shoulders.
2. Curl your toes into the floor and push your knees and hipbones up from the floor, pressing your tailbone backwards and upwards, spreading your weight amongst your hands rather than just the wrists.
3. Relax your neck and hold the pose for five breaths before letting your knees gently fall to the floor.

This is also a handy pose for getting your face a bit closer to the carpet and maybe seeing if it could do with a bit of a hoover.

DOWNWARD DOG ON THE WALL

This is a great alternative if you are not able to weight bear on your wrists.

1. Stand a few feet away from a wall and place your hands on the wall in front of you, shoulder height, fingers spread wide.
2. Move your feet back a little more so that they are slightly further back than your shoulders.
3. Extend the elbows a little and create some space between your shoulder blades, feeling more and more grounded into the wall as you're doing it.
4. Keeping your back and neck straight, start to sit into a squat slowly. Be sure not to arch your back, forming a straight line from your palms to your sit bones. Go only as far as you can to remain comfortable but in a stretch and pain-free.
5. If you feel like you can take it a step further, try to push a little more onto one arm whilst lifting the other one up slightly.

Stay there for a breath or two, lower your arm back down, and repeat on the other side.

6. To release the pose, move your weight back to the centre, towards your hips and legs and move both arms up from the wall, pushing yourself back up to a standing position.

DOWNWARD DOG WITH A CHAIR

To do the same pose with a chair, face the chair from a few feet away.

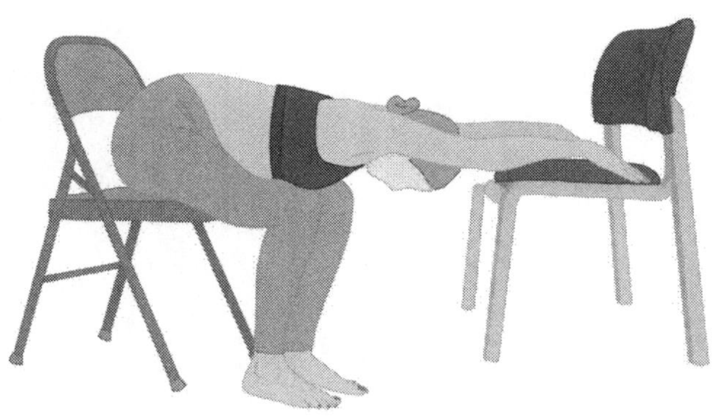

1. Bend forward and bring your hands to rest on the chair.
2. Press your hands into the chair and draw your hips back and try to drop your shoulders from your ears.
3. Imagine your tailbone being lifted high, as if it was attached by a piece of imaginary string to the ceiling.

We've completed a number of poses whilst sitting in the chair–now we are going to do some where you are standing but using the chair for support.

BACK STRETCH

1. Take a few steps back from your chair, inhale deeply then fold forward, resting your arms on the back of your chair.
2. Feel the weight in your arms and try to get a deep stretch.
3. When finished, slowly let your arms fall forward until you are in a forward fold.

FOOT TO SEAT POSE

Turn your chair so you're facing it from the side. Stand a couple of feet from the chair.

1. Place your left hand on the back of the chair and lift your right foot up onto the chair.

2. Depending on how flexible you are feeling, lift your right arm above your head, feeling the stretch, or place it on your hip.
3. Repeat on the other side.

Another variation on this pose:

1. Stand closer to the chair, lift and place your right foot on the chair seat, keeping your thigh parallel to the floor.
2. Place the right hand on your hip and your left hand on the right knee and twist to the right.
3. Don't put any pressure on your spine in this pose–the twist comes from the hips.
4. Repeat on the other side with the left foot on the chair.

TRIANGLE

This is a good pose to do when you are more flexible on the mat, but this variation with the chair is a nice spinal twist.

1. Stand with your feet three to four feet apart. On the foot furthest from the chair, turn the toes out at a 45-degree angle, with the toes of the other foot turned towards the chair.
2. Raise the arms to shoulder height whilst taking in a deep breath.
3. On the exhale, lower the arm closest to the chair down to the seat or the chair back, depending on your flexibility.
4. Look towards the ceiling but don't strain your neck when doing so.
5. Repeat on the other side.

EASY BALANCE POSE

Balancing in yoga is something that you have to practice continually. I've definitely improved over the years and using a chair (or wall) has really helped me. Keeping my attention on the breath, or picking a spot on the wall to look at, also helps me to retain my focus. But as always, don't worry if you stumble–just return to the pose, and always remember to breathe.

You can do this either facing the chair back or standing to the side–whichever position allows you to place one or both hands on the back of the chair, depending on how stable you feel. As you progress and develop your balance, you can ditch the chair completely, but keep it close by for those times when you have a bit of a wobble.

1. Looking straight ahead, shoulders over hips, raise your right foot off the ground in front of you, holding it for three breaths.

2. Return to the centre, before moving the right foot to one side for another three breaths.
3. Return it to the centre, before this time moving it behind you for a few more breaths.
4. Return to the centre and repeat on the other side.

MARCHING IN PLACE POSE

Let's stay with balance poses for the moment, as they are incredibly important in helping you to feel stable in your body, hopefully preventing injuries from falls. As well as being great for balance, this pose helps to strengthen ankles and calf muscles.

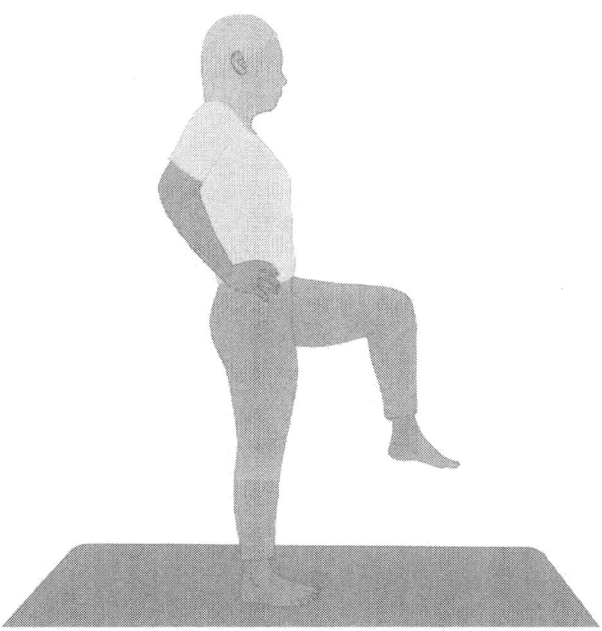

1. In this one, take up your mountain pose again.
2. Feel the connection to the ground with your left foot, really root down into it. On an inhale, with your hands placed on

your hips, lift your right knee as high as you can. Use a chair or a wall for balance if you need to.

3. On the exhale, gently place your right foot to the floor again.
4. Inhale, this time lifting your left knee and repeat five times on each side.

If you start to feel your balance improving and want to shake things up a little, try raising your arms at the same time you lift your knee.

STANDING ONE KNEE TO CHEST

Earlier we introduced you to this pose both on the mat and in the chair–this time we're going to do it standing up. Incidentally, any of the poses where you bring your knees to your chest are called 'the wind releasing pose.' If you have ever been in a yoga class, you often realise why this is aptly named, as the body moves toxins down then out through the body. Obviously, you don't have to worry about this if you are practicing home alone.

As well as helping with indigestion, this is a great strengthener for ankles, thighs, calves and spine, whilst also helping to both reduce pain and improve flexibility in the back.

As usual, keep a chair or wall close by if you need it for balance.

1. In your mountain pose, really root down into that left foot.
2. On an inhale, raise the right knee and locking your fingers around your shin, pull it towards your chest. Just use one

hand if you need to keep the other for balance. It's easy to automatically tense your shoulders here, so just let them drop down.

3. On the exhale, loosen the grip a little, then tighten again on the inhale.
4. See if you can hold this pose for five breaths like this and then repeat whilst standing on the right foot and lifting the left knee.

LEGS UP ON THE CHAIR

This is another deceptively simple pose that is incredibly beneficial, and that can also be done at the end of a session instead of savasana, which is listed below as the final pose.

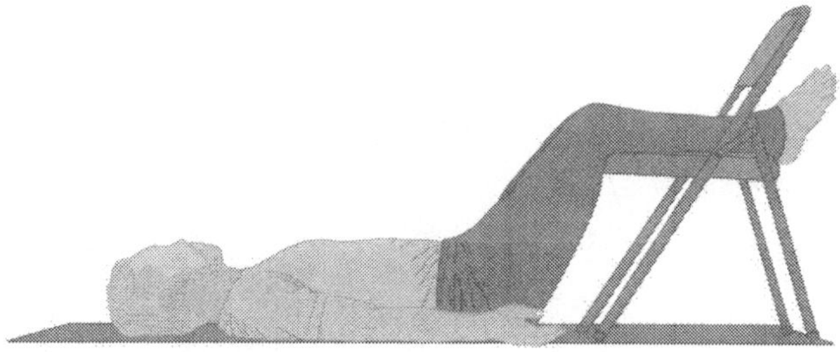

1. Lie on your back on the floor, with your legs bent and resting on the seat of the chair.

I've personally found this pose to be a great stress reliever–not sure how it works, but it may have something to do with the blood flowing to the top of the body. My friend Barry, a yoga teacher who I have mentioned earlier, likes to do this one with his feet against the wall, which works just as well. The ultimate pose to change the direction of your blood flow would be to stand on your head, but I haven't included it here as I don't think it qualifies as gentle yoga. If you do develop your practice and eventually end up standing on head, don't forget to turn your TV upside down as well so that you can enjoy your favourite programmes.

COBBLERS POSE

This is a popular pose that you will always encounter if you attend a yoga class. This is a great stretch, and really helps with opening up the hips and the groin–if you spend too much time sitting, you'll really feel the benefit of this one.

1. To do it, sit up tall on your mat with your spine nice and straight, drawing your feet in as close to your body as possible, whilst being aware of any pain (careful with this one

if you have any knee problems) and bring the soles of your feet together.

2. Don't force your knees to the ground, just let them rest naturally. Like a lot of poses in yoga, the more you practice, the greater flexibility you will notice. Feel free to put some extra padding under your sit bones if you need to.

A nice little bonus with this pose is to give your feet a bit of a massage. I personally think we don't show our feet enough love, so give them a rub when you're down there.

PLANK POSE

Before we move onto an actual yoga flow, which is where you move from one yoga pose into another in a continuous, smooth way (yes, you might as well be transforming into an expert yogi), we have to talk about a transitional pose that is used quite a lot in yoga. This is called the plank pose.

If you have problems with your wrists, you might want to skip this pose and refer to the modification below, where we complete the yoga flow–called the sun salutation–in a chair instead.

A strong core is essential for reducing stress on the joints and helping with posture. It's a great pose for strengthening your core and abdominal muscles, as well as your arms and legs, and will help balance and stability in everyday life. Be gentle with it to begin with, and remember to breathe during it. You'll surprise yourself at how adept you become in this pose.

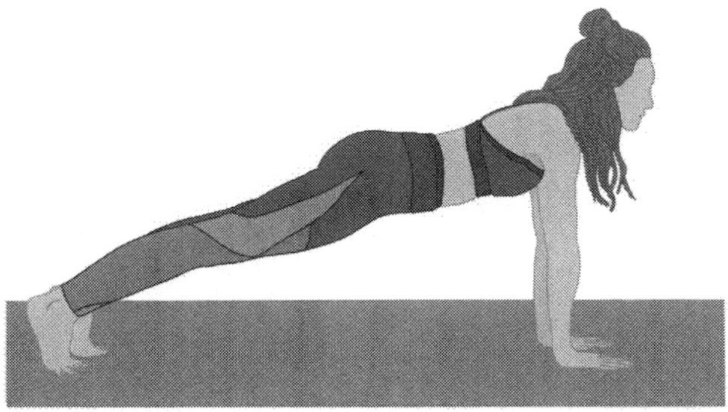

1. To get into the plank pose, place your hands on the mat, under the shoulders.
2. Step your feet back to the bottom of the mat, like you're about to start a push-up. That's it! You hold the pose here for a few breaths, around 30 seconds or whatever you can manage.

Feel your muscles engaging to keep your body in a straight line, especially in the abdomen, shoulders, core and legs. This is also a great opportunity to take a few moments to wonder when was the last time you swept the kitchen floor, to then simply draw your attention back to your breath. Stay in the pose for a few more seconds.

When you first try this, your bottom is likely to hike upwards or sag down low instead of keeping a straight line between the shoulders and heels. If this is impossible to achieve in the beginning, you should lower your knees on the floor. Feel free to use a blanket under your knees for that extra support. Keep your core engaged, and your torso at an incline, forming a straight line between your knees and your shoulders, with hips in the centre. Make sure not to arch your back and keep your head and neck in a straight line with your spine. Avoid hunching your shoulders too.

SUN SALUTATION

This is one of my favourite yoga flows, and as the name suggests, it's something I like to greet the day with. If I'm in a bit of a rush, I can do a few of these and feel nice and warmed up and ready to face the day. And if I've got a bit more time and am looking to get the whole body ready for a longer practice, this flow is a great place to start.

It's a great sequence for improving circulation, building strength and flexibility, boosting your metabolism, helping with weight loss, and improving stamina. Try to do ten of these in a row and you'll see what I mean.

It's also handy when I roll out the mat and don't know what I want to do. Very often I'll have a yoga book open, or a video sequence from one of my favourite yoga teachers on YouTube. One benefit of doing it along with a teacher from a video is that you don't feel so alone, and you can observe their movements as you go along, pausing and rewinding to make sure you're doing the pose correctly. The only drawback is that the teacher can't correct you if you're doing it wrong.

If you're OK with doing it on the mat, take your time learning the different movements. After a while, it becomes natural and you'll establish a rhythm between the different poses. I can't stress enough how important the breath is in this sequence, moving between poses either on an inhale or exhale. Or maybe you want to take your time, breathing in and out in each pose. Go at your own pace.

And now time for our traditional word of warning–avoid this pose if you have problems with or had surgery on your back, arms and shoulders.

And don't worry if you can't do this on the mat–we have a specially designed practice that you can do from the chair if you cannot bear weight on your hands.

Okay, so let's start with the sun salutation on the mat. Remember the mountain pose from earlier? Well, that's where we are starting, at the front of our mat.

1. Take an inhale and raise your arms above your head, palms coming together in a raised arms pose. Look upwards towards your thumbs and allow your shoulders to move upwards.

2. On the exhale, release your arms downwards and move into a forward bend. Bend your knees as much as you need to. Try to keep your fingertips in line with your toes, or as close to the ground as flexibility allows. I have mentioned using blocks before, and this is a good opportunity to use them if you need to, bringing the ground a bit closer to you.

3. On the inhale, lift your head into the flat back pose, moving your hands to your shins or coming on to your fingertips, whichever allows you to get a flat back.

4. Exhale and move into a plank pose, as described above, placing your hands on the mat, wrists under the shoulders. Step your feet back to the bottom of the mat into the 'push up' position. Keep your abdominal muscles engaged, drawing your navel towards your spine. Try not to arch your back or point your butt into the air, and imagine a straight line from the crown of your head to your toes. Try to keep your hips raised–it gets harder the longer you are in this pose. If you're struggling, don't worry–you can always drop your knees to the floor. We won't be here for long. Keep looking down at the floor and not tilted up so as not to strain your neck. Now take a deep inhale.

And exhale. When you're beginning to practice this pose, it's best to drop your chin, knees and chest to the floor, keeping your elbows hugging your ribs. After a while, when you've built up some core strength, you can let your body hover over the floor in what's called the four limbed staff pose. But this is gentle yoga, so we won't be worrying about that for now.

5. Inhaling, we move into a cobra pose. Careful with this one if you have any sort of spinal injury. Push your pelvis and the tops of your feet into the floor as you lift up through your chest and your arms. If the back bend feels too difficult, especially when you are starting off, bend your elbows as much as you need to (this is called a baby cobra). This is a great pose for reducing tension in the back and spine.

6. With an exhale, move into a downward dog. Feel free to take a few extra breaths here.

7. Now that you've been in a downward dog pose for a few breaths, exhale and move back to the standing forward bend here, fingertips touching the floor and bending the knees if you need to.

8. Inhale and move back into your mountain pose.

Well done, you have done a whole sun salutation!

First time moving from a cobra pose to a downward dog can be an awkward one, so don't worry if you aren't doing it quite as gracefully or don't have that much strength in your upper arms and shoulders as to push yourself up. You're more than welcome to get up from the cobra pose and assume a downward dog from a standing position, either on the mat or using the chair as aid. You're doing great. This is what we're all here for–to build strength and stability, for prosperity. If you can do everything perfectly first-off, well, you probably don't need a yoga book!

SUN SALUTATION WITH A CHAIR

Okay, so now we've done a standing sun salutation, we're going to try one that you can do from the chair. It's not going to be identical to the one on the mat, but the intention is to use as many different muscle groups as possible whilst aligning movements with the breath.

1. Let's start in the chair mountain pose. Sit up nice and straight, feet flat on the floor, hands resting gently in your lap.

2. Take an inhale as you reach for the sky, arms overhead with palms facing, fingers spread wide. Lift your gaze up but don't strain. Lift your ribs to find length in your spine.

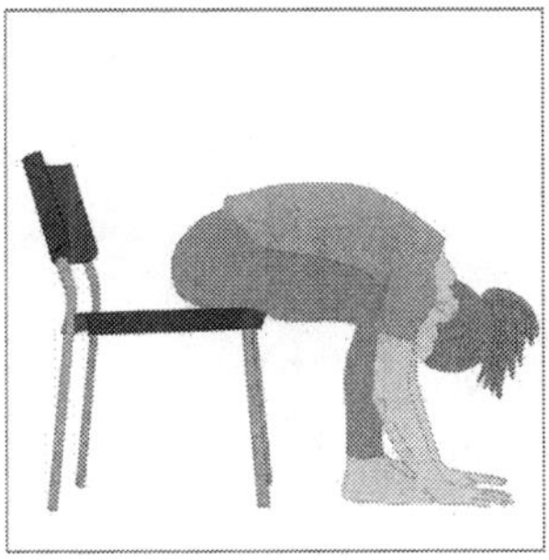

3. Exhale and fold forward over your legs, getting a good stretch. Let your head and shoulders hang loose towards the floor, letting your fingers touch the ground or bring the ground to you by using a yoga block (or a couple of books if you have them handy).

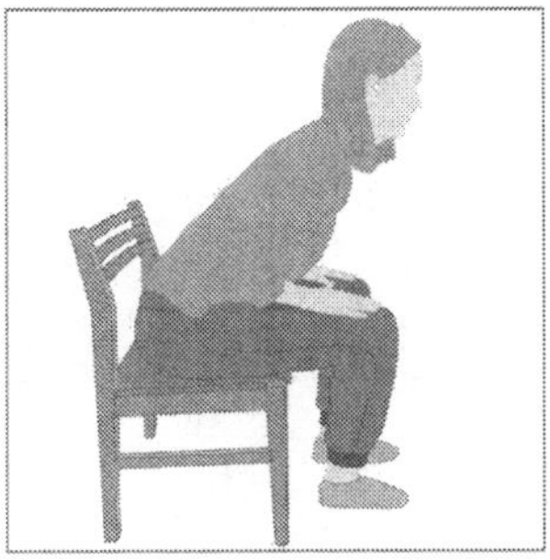

4. Take an inhale and lift your head and shoulders, trying to keep your back flat. Try and find a bit of length in your spine, from your tailbone through to the crown of your head.

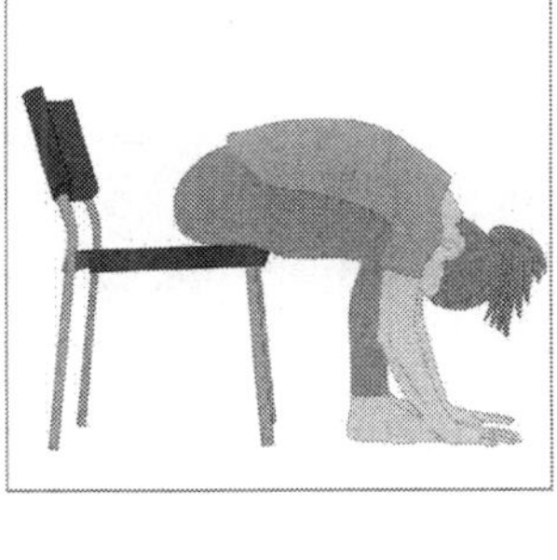

5. Exhale and go back into the same seated forward fold we mentioned earlier.

6. Next, we're going to take an inhale and move the arms overhead again.

7. Exhale and back to our seated mountain pose again.

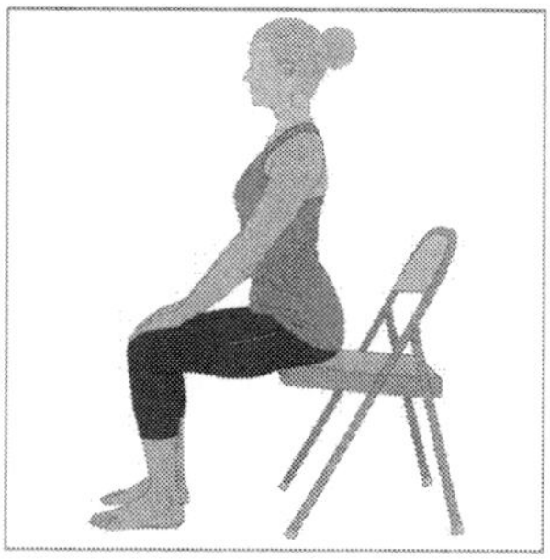

THE CORPSE POSE

One of my favourite yoga poses is the one I tend to finish my practice with, whether it's a quick ten-minute morning session or a more intense 45 minutes in the evening–the savasana, or corpse pose. It probably sounds easy, but it can be difficult, because you are relaxing, and not everyone finds that easy.

How to do it?

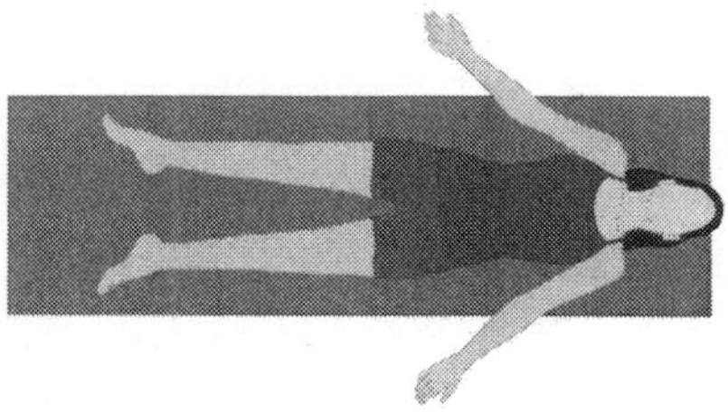

1. Lie on your mat.
2. Put a blanket underneath your head if you like, legs bent or extended, arms loosely spread out by your sides, palms facing upward.
3. Breathe deeply. Direct your attention towards all of your body's muscles, relaxing each group in turn. Start from the facial muscles, and move your attention slowly to the throat, then neck and shoulders, feeling any tension in there and letting it slowly fade away by allowing the muscles to relax. Can you feel how much tension you still hold in your neck and back, even when you thought you were lying down comfortably? Carry on and move onto your chest and upper arms, moving down to lower arms, paying attention to each part of your body for a few seconds as you move on to the next part, in this case, your hands and fingers. Move your attention back up to your torso, down to your hips, each leg, buttock, knee, foot and so on–the whole way around the body. Feeling the deep breaths move in and out, each part of the body feeling heavier and heavier. Our bodies keep a lot of tension, so we need to 'actively rest' to release it–who woulda thought?
4. Relax and let your breath move smoothly in and out for a few more breaths or as long as it takes. Try not to snore.

What's difficult about it? For me, I've generally never had a problem, as I can feel my body enjoying the fruits of my practice. But sometimes, especially if I have a stressful day ahead, I get tense just staring at the ceiling and want to get up!

But I don't, because I can always spare a minute for this pose, as it can often be the most beneficial one of my whole practice. It can also be easy to fall asleep, which might be OK if you are suffering from insomnia and have time on your hands, but perhaps not so good if you are supposed to be at work and you are snoozing on the floor. Or, your boss comes in and finds you snoozing on the floor, which is not a great look either.

No, what you are after here is what I would call a gentle alertness, remaining aware and relaxed. It's an exercise in 'letting go' which is different from our normal routine of constant 'doing'.

It's a great pose during times of stress. Relaxed and breathing deeply, move around your body and focus on each body part. Your yoga session should have already stretched the muscles and released some of the tension–it's amazing the amount of tension that we accumulate in our bodies, so by moving into each part we can really start to release this.

When I've attended classes, I've often noticed people skipping this pose, as they move off the mat, eager to get on with their day. I feel a great release with savasana, as my body and mind quieten. I don't mind saying that sometimes my savasana lasts as long as my yoga session! I think of it as a great gift to myself, as my nervous system allows itself to heal.

This is my go-to pose at night when I'm suffering from insomnia. Even better than doing it on the floor is to do it in bed, as you often find yourself falling asleep. Repeating this exercise seems to make it even more effective.

THE CORPSE POSE SEATED

If you're unable to lie on the floor, you can close your eyes and move your awareness around your body whilst sitting in a mountain pose. Starting from your head, move your attention to each body part in turn; take time to really notice the sensations from your forehead, cheeks, jaw and neck down to each shoulder and limb, all the way down to forearms and each finger, then the torso and so on, until you get to your feet, or do it in reverse.

~

VARIETY

I think you'll agree that there's a good variety in the poses featured and enough modifications to hopefully encourage everyone to have a go at them, whatever your ability, and be mindful of your own limitations. With the poses featured in this chapter and those in the previous sections, it should be possible for you to build a routine of ten to fifteen minutes each day.

Whilst the morning is a great time to do yoga, as it gives you a good boost as you start your day, afternoons are a good time too, especially to counteract that mid-afternoon slump that we experience as we get older. I especially like doing yoga in the afternoon as I've usually spent the morning sitting in the office, so it helps to give me a bit of an energy boost and releases pent-up energy and tension. Although we have emphasised the importance of establishing a practice of 15-20 minutes a day, there's nothing to stop you fitting in some of these exercises throughout your day, to suit your needs. After a while, when you have practised yoga for long enough, as I hope you will, your body will let you know when you need to do yoga.

The main point is to do little, but often. A 10 to 15-minute session a day is much more beneficial than practicing an hour once a week. Let your mind and body get used to yoga, let them grow into yoga, and soon you might find that you'll want to do more than 15 minutes at a time.

To keep things fresh, you can mix up how you perform these poses, and there are lots of other resources available online, if you're eager to take your yoga onto the next level and want to learn some new poses.

If you want recommendations on new poses to try, or connect with others, make sure to join a wonderful, private Facebook community called 'Beginner Yoga Poses' run by a lovely chap Tim Cormack. Type in the link below to your web browser or search for the group on Facebook.

And don't forget to claim your Free Gifts! The daily Yoga Planner and a printable version of all the poses in this book so you can mix and match them, plus a few extra poses. Feel free to stick these across the wall in your bedroom–next to your Monet or photos of your grandchildren. By claiming these free resources, you are automatically added to a mailing list. We won't be emailing you, but you will get added to the list so that we can send you the resources, plus an early copy of our next Chair Yoga book for free when it's out. You can leave the list any time you wish by a single click of a button. I promise–no spam, no sales, no hard feelings.

Free Gifts:

https://tinyurl.com/AdrianRose

Yoga community 'Beginner Yoga Poses' on Facebook:

https://www.facebook.com/groups/beginneryogaposes

9

CONCLUSION & USEFUL LINKS AND RESOURCES

I hope we have shown that yoga is a form of exercise that can help slow down the effects of ageing–and how many forms of exercise can say that? We've shown it to be accessible and, with some modifications, available to everyone in terms of ability; and a useful form of physical therapy for a variety of diseases and ailments.

We can't avoid old age or the possibility of illness. What we can do is prepare our bodies to deal with it as best we can. We can limit the damage of things like falling by strengthening both our bones and our balance.

Maybe you're not feeling any aches and pains now. But if I can ask you to do one thing for me, it is not to take your body for granted. A lot of the injuries occur because we're not using parts of our bodies–don't let that happen to you. No excuses, start now–you have the book in your hands, so you have the tools to get started. You can thank me later.

We've referred to a variety of studies and used a lot of statistics to show that a lot of what we have referred to in this book is backed up by research. Yoga has been around for 3000 years but it's only recently that we have been able to see just how effective it is from a scientific basis, and we can use this knowledge to improve our bodies.

I've included my own personal insights and experience throughout this book and writing it has been very much a labour of love for me. I've been a yoga practitioner for thirty years and I hope to be doing it into my old age. I consider myself so fortunate that I discovered that book on a shelf in the library all those years ago. To me, it was a blessing, as it's encouraged me to look after my body.

Yoga has been one of the greatest weapons in my arsenal. It has aided me as I overcome injury. It has helped me emotionally and mentally in many ways, in lots of different situations. Life is stressful, so we need all the help we can get.

My mam has also been a great source of inspiration to me, as I can see the incredible benefits that yoga has brought her. She is physically well, with a few aches and pains that come with age, but she lives with no physical restrictions and enjoys a full life at the age of 78. She was absolutely delighted when I told her I was writing this book and she hopes that you too can find yoga as rewarding as she has.

I didn't invent yoga–like I say, it's been around a couple of thousand years. But I am an enthusiast, advocate and practitioner of the ancient art and I hope I have persuaded some of you to give it a go. If there's a better exercise that works with the body, the heart and the mind, I have yet to find it.

If you've come this far in the book and haven't attempted any of the exercises, I'm not sure what else I can say to you. Only you can take the first step towards a better future YOU. There isn't going to be any big reveal here that pushes you forward, and if you're still lacking motivation, perhaps read the chapter on habit-forming again? Just try one pose and see what happens. Try another one the next day. The key is to just keep at it, even when you don't feel like it, because your body will thank you.

Maybe you're a bit cautious, and worried about injury–that's okay, it's absolutely natural. Speak to your doctor first and try some of the simpler ones mentioned in the earlier chapters.

Perhaps you'd prefer the reassurance and guidance of an experienced yoga teacher and that's great–you could search for classes in your area. Maybe that will give you the confidence to come back and start practising in your home. Or, you could join an online Yoga Basics Challenge by an experienced yoga teacher, such as Jennifer Forck-Powless, to kick start your yoga journey. Her challenge is aimed at those who are a little stuck and don't know how to start a home yoga practice, which you can access via the link at the bottom. The challenge is a 3-day mix of live Q&A and recorded content. What's 3 days to truly get on board with yoga, and that with guidance from a 500-hour yoga instructor? A 500-hour training is the highest international standard for yoga teachers including hundreds of hours of hands-on experience.

Alternatively to a live class, I can recommend 'Yoga for Adrienne' as a great, free resource on YouTube to learn some new poses as well as practice those we have detailed here. She has many videos, including those for seniors and people with disabilities and various conditions. If you have osteoporosis or osteopenia, be sure to check out Dr Loren Fishman's channel on YouTube, the physician who incorporates yoga into his treatment plans for patients. The video is called 'Dr Fishman's Method – 12 Poses vs Osteoporosis', which you can Google or type into YouTube.

Yoga with Kassandra is also a good online teacher, and I would recommend her 30 days of yoga in the evening as a great course to do before you go to bed. Yoga in the evening is a great way of winding down, of letting go of the stresses and strains of the day. I don't think it's possible to underestimate the power of a good night's sleep in helping with restoring our health. Finishing with savasana whilst lying in bed is a great way to drop off into the land of nod.

Yoga is of great benefit at any age, I can vouch for that, as can my mother. Whatever stage you're at, I hope what you have read inspires you to start your own yoga practice, as it is a personal journey for each of us. It's rewarding, beneficial and offers great benefits for your body, your mind and your heart.

Do join the 'Beginner Yoga Poses' Facebook group for that extra push and motivation, lots of useful tips on beginner yoga, suggestions for poses, or to simply connect with other people from all over the world who are on the same journey as you. If you ever have a question about anything, you can post it in the group and you'll be guaranteed to get lots of helpful replies and suggestions from other experienced practitioners or teachers who are part of the group. It's a truly wonderful community. You'll be able to read many inspirational stories about how yoga has changed the lives of people like me and you. Do go and take a look.

I wish you well in your journey and thank you for reading. If you have enjoyed the book, it would be extremely beneficial if you could leave a review on Amazon. Reviews are the bread and butter for small authors like us. I hope you agree that the more people that can read this book the better, as there are many out there who perhaps don't know where to start, and this book can be the first stepping stone on a wonderful journey.

I wish you well in your journey and thank you for reading. I send you light and love and *namaste*.

Get in touch & Useful Links:

Free Gifts: https://tinyurl.com/AdrianRose

Recommended Facebook group:
Beginner Yoga Poses run by Tim Cormack
https://www.facebook.com/groups/beginneryogaposes

Join Tim's mailing list to receive a helpful free guide to beginner yoga:
https://beginneryogaposes.co/beginners-guide/

Jennifer's 3 day Yoga Basics Challenge:
http://truetoyouyoga.com
https://www.facebook.com/groups/truetoyouyogawithjennifermarie

Email me: contact@adrianroseyoga.com

REFERENCES

12 Minutes of Yoga For Stronger Bones. (2015, December 21). The New York Times. Retrieved May 25, 2022, from https://well.blogs.nytimes.com/2015/12/21/12-minutes-of-yoga-for-stronger-bones/?_r=0

50 Blissful Yoga Statistics for 2022. (2022, January 7). Yoga Earth. Retrieved June 13, 2022, from https://yogaearth.com/yoga-research/yoga-statistics/

Age UK. (2018a, September 25). *All the Lonely People: Loneliness in Later Life*. Retrieved June 12, 2022, from https://www.ageuk.org.uk/latest-press/articles/2018/october/all-the-lonely-people-report/

Age UK. (2018b, December 14). *Christmas loneliness statistics*. Retrieved June 12, 2022, from https://www.ageuk.org.uk/latest-press/articles/2018/december/christmas-loneliness-statistics/

April/June 2016–Volume 32–Issue 2 : Topics in Geriatric Rehabilitation. (2016, June). Topics in Geriatric Rehabilitation. https://journals.lww.com/topicsingeriatricrehabilitation/Fulltext/2016/04000/

Blackwell, D. L., & Clarke, T. C. (2018, June). *State Variation in Meeting the 2008 Federal Guidelines for Both Aerobic and Muscle-strengthening Activities Through Leisure-time Physical Activity Among Adults Aged 18–644: United States, 2010–2015.* U.S. Department of Health and Human Services. https://www.cdc.gov/nchs/data/nhsr/nhsr112.pdf

BoneSmart Pilates. (2021, December 15). *How to Modify the Cat-cow Exercise* [Video]. YouTube. https://www.youtube.com/watch?v=spmLiWAv2Lo

Centers for Disease Control and Prevention. (2015, November). *Wellness-related Use of Common Complementary Health Approaches Among Adults: United States, 2012.* U.S. Department of Health and Human Services. https://www.cdc.gov/nchs/data/nhsr/nhsr085.pdf

Centers for Disease Control and Prevention. (2018, June). *General Physical Activities Defined by Level of Intensity.* U.S. Department of Health and Human Services. https://www.cdc.gov/nccdphp/dnpa/physical/pdf/pa_intensity_table_2_1.pdf

Central Health Education Unit. (2012). *Recommendations for Prescribing Exercise to Overweight and Obese Patients.* Https://Www.Chp.Gov.Hk/Archive/Epp/Files/DoctorsHanbook_ch10.Pdf. https://www.chp.gov.hk/archive/epp/files/DoctorsHanbook_ch10.pdf

Chair Yoga More Effective than Music in Adults with Advanced Dementia. (2019, October 2). Florida Atlantic University. https://www.fau.edu/newsdesk/articles/chair-yoga-dementia.php

Chu, P., Gotink, R. A., Yeh, G. Y., Goldie, S. J., & Hunink, M. M. (2014). The effectiveness of yoga in modifying risk factors for cardiovascular disease and metabolic syndrome: A systematic review and meta-analysis of randomized controlled trials. *European Journal of Preventive Cardiology, 23*(3). https://doi.org/10.1177/2047487314562741

Clear, J. (2020, February 4). *Habit Stacking: How to Build New Habits by Taking Advantage of Old Ones*. James Clear. https://jamesclear.-com/habit-stacking

Donnelly Michos, E. (2021, August 8). *Sitting Disease: How a Sedentary Lifestyle Affects Heart Health*. Johns Hopkins Medicine. Retrieved June 13, 2022, from https://www.hopkinsmedicine.org/health/wellness-and-prevention/sitting-disease-how-a-sedentary-lifestyle-affects-heart-health

Dr. Fishman's Method– 12 Poses vs Osteporosis. (2016, September 18). [Video]. YouTube. https://www.youtube.com/watch?v=o8SjystaH-E&t=1094s

Exercise: The miracle cure and the role of the doctor in promoting it. (2015, February). Academy of Medical Royal Colleges. https://www.aomr-c.org.uk/wp-content/uploads/2016/05/Exercise_the_Mira-cle_Cure_0215.pdf

Fishman, L. (2022, January 17). *The Practice: The Fishman Method—Yoga for Osteoporosis*. The Art of Living Retreat Center. https://artoflivin-gretreatcenter.org/blog/fishman-method-yoga-osteoporosis/

How Do I Increase My Synovial Fluid? (2022, January 13). Verywell Health. https://www.verywellhealth.com/how-to-increase-synovial-fluid-5114374

Handschin, C., & Spiegelman, B. M. (2008). The role of exercise and PGC1α in inflammation and chronic disease. *Nature, 454*(7203), 469. https://doi.org/10.1038/nature07206

Harvard Health. (2015, April 29). Yoga for pain relief. https://www.health.harvard.edu/alternative-and-integrative-health/yoga-for-pain-relief

How Your Joints Benefit From Exercise. (2015, August 26). Living With Arthritis. http://blog.arthritis.org/living-with-arthritis/exercise-benefits-for-joints/

Hunter, D. J., March, L., & Chew, M. (2020). Osteoarthritis in 2020 and beyond: a Lancet Commission. *The Lancet, 396*(10264). https://doi.org/10.1016/s0140-6736(20)32230-3

Jandre Reis, F. J., & Macedo, A. R. (2015). Influence of Hamstring Tightness in Pelvic, Lumbar and Trunk Range of Motion in Low Back Pain and Asymptomatic Volunteers during Forward Bending. *Asian Spine Journal, 9*(4). https://doi.org/10.4184/asj.2015.9.4.535

Kravitz, L. (n.d.). *From 1998 to 2011: ACSM Publishes Updated Exercise Guidelines*. The University of New Mexico. https://www.unm.edu/~lkravitz/Article%20folder/ACSMGuidelinesUNM.pdf

Lally, P., van Jaarsveld, C. H. M., Potts, H. W. W., & Wardle, J. (2009). How are habits formed: Modelling habit formation in the real world. *European Journal of Social Psychology, 40*(6). https://doi.org/10.1002/ejsp.674

Lu, Y. H., Rosner, B., Chang, G., & Fishman, L. M. (2016). Twelve-Minute Daily Yoga Regimen Reverses Osteoporotic Bone Loss. *Topics in Geriatric Rehabilitation, 32*(2). https://doi.org/10.1097/tgr.0000000000000085

McKendry, J. (2019, August 30). *Comparable Rates of Integrated Myofibrillar Protein Synthesis Between Endurance-Trained Master Athletes and Untrained Older Individuals*. Frontiers. Retrieved June 12, 2022, from https://www.frontiersin.org/articles/10.3389/fphys.2019.01084/full

Mualem, R. (2018). *The Effect of Movement on Cognitive Performance*. Frontiers. https://www.frontiersin.org/articles/10.3389/fpubh.2018.00100/full

Park, J. H., Moon, J. H., Kim, H. J., Kong, M. H., & Oh, Y. H. (2020). Sedentary Lifestyle: Overview of Updated Evidence of Potential Health Risks. *Korean Journal of Family Medicine, 41*(6). https://doi.org/10.4082/kjfm.20.0165

Physical inactivity a leading cause of disease and disability, warns WHO. (2002, April 4). World Health Organization. Retrieved June 13, 2022, from https://www.who.int/news/item/04-04-2002-physical-inactivity-a-leading-cause-of-disease-and-disability-warns-who

Saint-Maurice, P. F., PhD. (2022, March 1). *Estimated Number of Deaths Prevented Through Increased Physical Activity Among US Adults*. Cardiology | JAMA Internal Medicine | JAMA Network. Retrieved June 12, 2022, from https://jamanetwork.com/journals/jamainternalmedicine/fullarticle/2788473

Shete, S., Verma, A., & Doddoli, G. (2020). Yoga therapy for fibromyalgia syndrome: A case report. *Journal of Family Medicine and Primary Care, 9*(1), 435. https://doi.org/10.4103/jfmpc.jfmpc_816_19

Sivakumar, P., Hariprasad, V., Koparde, V., Varambally, S., Thirthalli, J., Varghese, M., Basavaraddi, I., & Gangadhar, B. (2013). Randomized clinical trial of yoga-based intervention in residents from elderly homes: Effects on cognitive function. *Indian Journal of Psychiatry, 55*(7). https://doi.org/10.4103/0019-5545.116308

Stress: are we coping? (2020, January 16). Mental Health Foundation. https://www.mentalhealth.org.uk/publications/stress-are-we-coping

Thirthalli, J., Naveen, G., Rao, M., Varambally, S., Christopher, R., & Gangadhar, B. (2013). Cortisol and antidepressant effects of yoga. *Indian Journal of Psychiatry, 55*(7). https://doi.org/10.4103/0019-5545.116315

Tiwari, S., Dutt, K., Kumar, R., Dhananjai, S., & Sadashiv. (2013). Reducing psychological distress and obesity through Yoga practice. *International Journal of Yoga, 6*(1). https://doi.org/10.4103/0973-6131.105949

Volpi, E., Nazemi, R., & Fujita, S. (2004). Muscle tissue changes with aging. *Current Opinion in Clinical Nutrition and Metabolic Care, 7*(4). https://doi.org/10.1097/01.mco.0000134362.76653.b2

Why Our Brains Are Hardwired to Focus on the Negative. (2020, April 30). Verywell Mind. https://www.verywellmind.com/negative-bias-4589618

The Yoga-Heart Connection. (2021, December 2). Johns Hopkins Medicine. https://www.hopkinsmedicine.org/health/wellness-and-prevention/the-yoga-heart-connection

NOTES

2. WHAT HAPPENS WHEN YOU MIX OLD AGE AND EXERCISE? YOU'LL BE SHOCKED

1. Handschin, C., & Spiegelman, B. M. (2008). The role of exercise and PGC1α in inflammation and chronic disease. *Nature, 454*(7203), 469. https://doi.org/10.1038/nature07206
2. McKendry, J. (2019, August 30). *Comparable Rates of Integrated Myofibrillar Protein Synthesis Between Endurance-Trained Master Athletes and Untrained Older Individuals*. Frontiers. Retrieved June 12, 2022, from https://www.frontiersin.org/articles/10.3389/fphys.2019.01084/full
3. Saint-Maurice, P. F., PhD. (2022b, March 1). *Estimated Number of Deaths Prevented Through Increased Physical Activity Among US Adults*. Cardiology | JAMA Internal Medicine | JAMA Network. https://jamanetwork.com/journals/jamainternalmedicine/fullarticle/2788473
4. Kravitz, L. (n.d.). *From 1998 to 2011: ACSM Publishes Updated Exercise Guidelines*. The University of New Mexico. https://www.unm.edu/~lkravitz/Article%20folder/ACSMGuidelinesUNM.pdf
5. Volpi, E., Nazemi, R., & Fujita, S. (2004). Muscle tissue changes with aging. *Current Opinion in Clinical Nutrition and Metabolic Care, 7*(4). https://doi.org/10.1097/01.mco.0000134362.76653.b2
6. Lu, Y. H., Rosner, B., Chang, G., & Fishman, L. M. (2016). Twelve-Minute Daily Yoga Regimen Reverses Osteoporotic Bone Loss. *Topics in Geriatric Rehabilitation, 32*(2). https://doi.org/10.1097/tgr.0000000000000085
7. Age UK. (2018a, September 25). All the Lonely People: Loneliness in Later Life. Retrieved June 12, 2022, from https://www.ageuk.org.uk/latest-press/articles/2018/october/all-the-lonely-people-report/
8. Age UK. (2018b, December 14). *Christmas loneliness statistics*. Retrieved June 12, 2022, from https://www.ageuk.org.uk/latest-press/articles/2018/december/christmas-loneliness-statistics/

3. WHY EVERYTHING YOU KNOW ABOUT YOGA MIGHT BE WRONG

1. *50 Blissful Yoga Statistics for 2022.* (2022, January 7). Yoga Earth. Retrieved June 13, 2022, from https://yogaearth.com/yoga-research/yoga-statistics/
2. Jandre Reis, F. J., & Macedo, A. R. (2015). Influence of Hamstring Tightness in Pelvic, Lumbar and Trunk Range of Motion in Low Back Pain and Asymptomatic

Volunteers during Forward Bending. *Asian Spine Journal, 9*(4). https://doi.org/10.4184/asj.2015.9.4.535

3. *How Your Joints Benefit From Exercise.* (2015, August 26). Living With Arthritis. http://blog.arthritis.org/living-with-arthritis/exercise-benefits-for-joints/

4. WHY IS IT MORE DANGEROUS TO STAY SEDENTARY AND WHAT CAN YOU DO ABOUT IT NOW

1. *Physical inactivity a leading cause of disease and disability, warns WHO.* (2002, April 4). World Health Organization. Retrieved June 13, 2022, from https://www.who.int/news/item/04-04-2002-physical-inactivity-a-leading-cause-of-disease-and-disability-warns-who
2. Park, J. H., Moon, J. H., Kim, H. J., Kong, M. H., & Oh, Y. H. (2020). Sedentary Lifestyle: Overview of Updated Evidence of Potential Health Risks. *Korean Journal of Family Medicine, 41*(6). https://doi.org/10.4082/kjfm.20.0165
3. Donnelly Michos, E. (2021, August 8). *Sitting Disease: How a Sedentary Lifestyle Affects Heart Health.* Johns Hopkins Medicine. Retrieved June 13, 2022, from https://www.hopkinsmedicine.org/health/wellness-and-prevention/sitting-disease-how-a-sedentary-lifestyle-affects-heart-health
4. Mualem, R. (2018). *The Effect of Movement on Cognitive Performance.* Frontiers. https://www.frontiersin.org/articles/10.3389/fpubh.2018.00100/full
5. Blackwell, D. L., & Clarke, T. C. (2018, June). *State Variation in Meeting the 2008 Federal Guidelines for Both Aerobic and Muscle-strengthening Activities Through Leisure-time Physical Activity Among Adults Aged 18–644: United States, 2010–2015.* U.S. Department of Health and Human Services. https://www.cdc.gov/nchs/data/nhsr/nhsr112.pdf
6. Centers for Disease Control and Prevention. (2018, June). *General Physical Activities Defined by Level of Intensity.* U.S. Department of Health and Human Services. https://www.cdc.gov/nccdphp/dnpa/physical/pdf/pa_intensity_table_2_1.pdf

5. THE EASIEST WAY TO TURN YOGA INTO A DAILY HABIT

1. Lally, P., van Jaarsveld, C. H. M., Potts, H. W. W., & Wardle, J. (2009). How are habits formed: Modelling habit formation in the real world. *European Journal of Social Psychology, 40*(6). https://doi.org/10.1002/ejsp.674
2. *Why Our Brains Are Hardwired to Focus on the Negative.* (2020, April 30). Verywell Mind. https://www.verywellmind.com/negative-bias-4589618

6. WHY WE MIGHT NOT BE BREATHING CORRECTLY & HOW YOGA CAN HELP WHEN THE GOING GETS TOUGH

1. *Stress: are we coping?* (2020, January 16). Mental Health Foundation. https://www.-mentalhealth.org.uk/publications/stress-are-we-coping

7. IS YOGA GOING TO MAKE MY EXISTING CONDITION WORSE?

1. Hunter, D. J., March, L., & Chew, M. (2020). Osteoarthritis in 2020 and beyond: a Lancet Commission. *The Lancet, 396*(10264). https://doi.org/10.1016/s0140-6736(20)32230-3
2. Lu, Y. H., Rosner, B., Chang, G., & Fishman, L. M. (2016). Twelve-Minute Daily Yoga Regimen Reverses Osteoporotic Bone Loss. *Topics in Geriatric Rehabilitation, 32*(2). https://doi.org/10.1097/tgr.0000000000000085
3. *Exercise: The miracle cure and the role of the doctor in promoting it.* (2015, February). Academy of Medical Royal Colleges. https://www.aomrc.org.uk/wp-content/uploads/2016/05/Exercise_the_Miracle_Cure_0215.pdf
4. *Harvard Health. (2015, April 29). Yoga for pain relief. https://www.health.harvard.edu/alternative-and-integrative-health/yoga-for-pain-relief*
5. *Chair Yoga More Effective than Music in Adults with Advanced Dementia.* (2019, October 2). Florida Atlantic University. https://www.fau.edu/newsdesk/articles/chair-yoga-dementia.php
6. Sivakumar, P., Hariprasad, V., Koparde, V., Varambally, S., Thirthalli, J., Varghese, M., Basavaraddi, I., & Gangadhar, B. (2013). Randomized clinical trial of yoga-based intervention in residents from elderly homes: Effects on cognitive function. *Indian Journal of Psychiatry, 55*(7). https://doi.org/10.4103/0019-5545.116308
7. Shete, S., Verma, A., & Doddoli, G. (2020). Yoga therapy for fibromyalgia syndrome: A case report. *Journal of Family Medicine and Primary Care, 9*(1), 435. https://doi.org/10.4103/jfmpc.jfmpc_816_19
8. *Exercise: The miracle cure and the role of the doctor in promoting it.* (2015, February). Academy of Medical Royal Colleges. https://www.aomrc.org.uk/wp-content/uploads/2016/05/Exercise_the_Miracle_Cure_0215.pdf
9. Thirthalli, J., Naveen, G., Rao, M., Varambally, S., Christopher, R., & Gangadhar, B. (2013). Cortisol and antidepressant effects of yoga. *Indian Journal of Psychiatry, 55*(7). https://doi.org/10.4103/0019-5545.116315
10. Chu, P., Gotink, R. A., Yeh, G. Y., Goldie, S. J., & Hunink, M. M. (2014). The effectiveness of yoga in modifying risk factors for cardiovascular disease and metabolic syndrome: A systematic review and meta-analysis of randomized controlled trials. *European Journal of Preventive Cardiology, 23*(3). https://doi.org/10.1177/2047487314562741
11. Central Health Education Unit. (2012). *Recommendations for Prescribing Exercise to Overweight and Obese Patients.* Https://Www.Chp.Gov.Hk/Archive/Epp/Files/Doc-

torsHanbook_ch10.Pdf. https://www.chp.gov.hk/archive/epp/files/DoctorsHanbook_ch10.pdf

12. Tiwari, S., Dutt, K., Kumar, R., Dhananjai, S., & Sadashiv. (2013). Reducing psychological distress and obesity through Yoga practice. *International Journal of Yoga, 6*(1). https://doi.org/10.4103/0973-6131.105949
13. Centers for Disease Control and Prevention. (2015, November). *Wellness-related Use of Common Complementary Health Approaches Among Adults: United States, 2012.* U.S. Department of Health and Human Services. https://www.cdc.gov/nchs/data/nhsr/nhsr085.pdf

Printed in Dunstable, United Kingdom

76458178R00089